CPSIA information can be obtained
at www.ICGtesting.com
Printed in the USA
BVHW031109210520
580083BV00005B/30

Unexpected:
Five Inspirational Short Stories of Encouragement

JOZUA VAN OTTERLOO

UNEXPECTED
FIVE INSPIRATIONAL SHORT STORIES OF ENCOURAGEMENT

Cardinia Ranges Publishing House
Beaconsfield, Victoria 3807, Australia

Unexpected: Five Inspirational Short Stories of Encouragement
Copyright ©2020 by Jozua van Otterloo
First published 2020

ISBN: 978-0-6484203-0-9 (Hardcover edition)
ISBN: 978-0-6484203-1-6 (Paperback edition)
ISBN: 978-0-6484203-2-3 (eBook: EPUB edition)
ISBN: 978-0-6484203-3-0 (eBook: MOBI and Kindle edition)

A catalogue record for this book is available from the National Library of Australia

Cover: photograph of a gray squirrel in the Grand Canyon, AZ. Picture and design: Jozua van Otterloo.
Interior design: Jozua van Otterloo

To my wonderful Andria

Contents

Preface

Ever since I was a young child, I have always loved stories. I loved to listen to them and I loved telling them. I liked to write my own stories and share them with my family, friends and classmates. Most stories I wrote as a school-aged child had a purpose. I never liked telling a story without a moral; there needed to be a message or a call to action.

Moving into the realm of universities and academia, the stories ended on the backburner. Being a geologist, all writing must be accurate and concise. Story telling is limited in taking the expert reader on a journey from why this study? what did we find? and what does it mean? There is no space for painting a picture of the scene in which the story is situated (other than a factual geologic background section with lots of references to the scientific literature), or describing emotions; something that would make the text more relatable.

With this book, I want to pick up the art of story telling again, and just like before, I like to convey a message through my stories. There is no better message than to spur people on to be people of encouragement. With this book I would like to encourage and inspire our generation, and the next, to be known as encouragers, those that went out of their way to make life better for those around them.

Please note, it is not an academic piece of work. It is solely written to inspire and encourage regardless of educational or religious background. However, I did include footnotes, as I believe that when referring to other stories, or someone else's ideas, it is good to provide the sources of that material. I strongly believe that the reader should always be able to check and judge how true and valid the text and its sources are – maybe this is the academic side in me popping up.

I hope you enjoy reading this book with its stories and personal reflections just as much as I did writing it.

Jozua van Otterloo, May 2020

PREFACE

Introduction

"I expect to pass through this life but once. If, therefore, there be any kindness I can show,
or any good thing I can do to any fellow being, let me do it now, for I shall not pass this
way again."
William Penn

Unexpected encouragement. How often have we found ourselves in a situation where we felt stuck, overwhelmed, or completely opposite, ready to go venture out and make a mark on the world? How often have we found ourselves in such a situation, but those around us didn't seem to care, or didn't seem to understand the weight or significance of it all. To them, it seemed, it all was just a small effort, a little thing, nothing to be bothered about.

In those moments, when we seemed to tackle life on our own, how different were the words of encouragement spoken to us, unexpectedly? How different were those acts that told us that, what was on our plate, was significant. What we were facing, it mattered.

Those encouraging words or acts were like little pockets packed with unimaginably powerful energy. They touched us and something changed within us. We found a charge. The mountain no longer seemed unsurmountable. The valley no longer seemed so deep.

Encouragement – it is one of the most powerful forces at work in our lives. But what is it? As a scientist, I'd love to measure, pinpoint and describe exactly what, where and how much. However, encouragement doesn't let itself be measured, pinned down or described numerically. It is a matter between hearts of a people; it is a force existing in the exchange between people.

It can be freely created and given, and it can be withheld and withdrawn. Only the giver and receiver totally understand the depth and strength of the exchange. Everyone else standing by can only merely guess.

Encouragement – it is a powerful force existing in the exchange between people. But what is it, exactly?

It is a word originating from Latin and passed into English by the French. Encouragement – it has the words *en* (within) and *courage* (from the Latin *cor*, 'heart'). It essentially means literally 'to place/build courage within' or even 'to place a heart within in', to hearten.

Although Latin and Roman thought have shaped Western thinking in an undeniably significant way, Latin-speaking Romans were influenced by other languages and cultural philosophies. They massively drew from the Greeks, albeit that they lost the subtlety of the eastern Mediterranean cultures in the process.

In Koine Greek, the language at the time of the most productive exchange between the Greeks and the Romans, encouragement is known as *paraklein*. This word is deeper than just 'placing courage within', it means to 'come alongside someone'. It is not static, but it is organic. It is relational. It occurs when someone chooses to make someone else important enough to at least journey together for a short period of time.

The third word giving meaning to encouragement comes from further east than ancient Greece: the Levantine region. It still is important to us since Western thought is grounded in the roots of Judeao-Christian principles. Hebrew is the formative language of these principles.

Ancient Hebrew didn't contain a specific noun that we can overlay the modern concept of encouragement with, however, it did contain a word that among other meanings, also provided the meaning of this. The word is *chazaq* (pronounced *khawzak*) and means 'to strengthen, to hold firm or to encourage'. In its root form it only has three letters: *chet*, *zayin* and *qoph*.

Hebrew, an ancient and intricate language was written down long before any of the European languages were. The letters don't just give us sounds, but they are pictures that tell stories in and of themselves.

- The *chet* is the picture of a fence, which divides and separates but also protects and keeps inside.
- The *zayin* is the picture of a plough or a weapon, which carries with it hard work to till the land, or fighting force to defend it.
- Lastly, the *qoph* is more personable, as it is the picture of the back of someone's head, like a head turning. The qoph tells us something about moving away, changing focus, following a different direction.

Chet – zayin – qoph. Fence – plough/weapon – back of a head.

It tells us the deeper story of a person working hard, or even fighting, to hold on, to protect, by changing focus, by following a different direction, or even the guidance of another person. Something or someone speaks into our lives and helps us to hold on, to work hard and to fight for the cause placed in our care, whatever this may be.

This book is all about that. It is about inspiring us to become encouragers to others, whomever we find on our path. *To place courage within them, by coming along side them and inspiring them to hold on, to work hard, to fight for the cause placed in their care.*

Just as encouragement doesn't let itself be measured or described using modern science. I have decided to divert from modern reasoning and to apply a more ancient form of exchange and explanation. I like to inspire us through the ancient art of storytelling.

Stories have inspired so many of us for thousands of years, and they continue to do so. Some stories are merely to entertain or place a smile on someone's face. However, most stories have deeper meaning, as they were passed on with a greater purpose[1].

Some stories have been shared on their own around a campfire. Others have been shared like poems from a sage teaching younger disciples. Some stories carried news from kingdoms far away, others conveyed thoughts that dealt with realms beyond our own observations.

There are many different types of stories. One particular type of story is the parable. It can be a longer story, or is just a short one-sentence comparison. Nonetheless, it brings an image to someone's mind, whether it be simple or highly intricate. This image, then, takes us to a familiar place and draws us to a deeper meaning that is often unfamiliar or hard to describe.

Aristotle and Plato used parables to explain greater wisdom to their pupils[2]. Ancient Hebrew prophets, and, in their tradition, later Jewish Rabbis used parables to pass on or explain a message from God[3].

Jesus of Nazareth is probably the best-known teller of parables. Sometimes his parables have been meticulously pieced apart to find metaphors with deeper hidden meanings that were not warranted by the actual stories. Later scholars, therefore, have rejected any form of allegorizing[4] but in the process lost their way in what parables were actually meant to do, to draw us using familiar images into a deeper but often unfamiliar truth.

I am not likening myself to Jesus, or my stories to his parables. However, I think he was onto something. He managed to describe and inspire such deep motivation by using such a simple tool. He showed us the power of storytelling and, in particular, the telling of parables.

My short stories in a sense are like parables. Using these, I want to describe different forms of encouragement, and inspire us to harness and use its power to build up others around us.

Importantly, when reading or hearing parables, you should always keep an eye on these questions[5]:

- Where would I fit in the story? Could I be one of the people, if so who, or am I a bystander like the narrator?
- What stands out to me in the story? Is it weird, shocking, or enlightening?
- What is the meaning of the story? What is its specific purpose?
- What would it want me to do? What is the inspiration or call to action?

As no parable should stand on its own, I also give a personal reflection on each story. I share a few of my personal thoughts and experiences, but I won't leave the matter ungrounded. I also share some findings from others who have studied various aspects at a deeper level than I.

At the end of this book, I have also placed a few tools that can practically help us in becoming people of encouragement.

My hope and intent are that this book as a whole, but also each story, reflection and poem individually, touches you, inspires you and empowers you to become a true encourager. My personal wish is that this world will be filled with *more* encouragers. After all, all it takes is a *single* encourager that can make the difference in another's person life, and support and motivate them to develop and bring about a medicine, a technology, a scientific discovery, that can alter the lives of many for good.

Will you join me and become an encourager?

"Little deeds of kindness,
Little words of love,
Help to make earth happy
Like the heaven above."
Julia Fletcher Carney

"Therefore encourage one another and build each other up, just as in fact you are doing."
1 Thessalonians 5:11, NIV.

Food for Thought

"Everybody has problems, but everybody also has blessings in life."
Robert W. Bly, *Count Your Blessings*

Unexpected. Encouragement is like a river flowing under a bridge, like those you would see in most cities around the world. A wide bridge, with a major road on top running into or out of the city, as well as paths for cyclists and pedestrians. Under its archways the river is contained by steep, concrete banks alongside one of these banks a pathway runs from one side of the bridge to the other. Some greenery on either side makes the place more serene and gives it a sense of being hidden from the every-day business happening just thirty feet above.

The river, made up of millions upon millions of water droplets, flows under this bridge. Some of it touches the concrete banks, but most of it flows fast following the river channel laid out before it. Where the river goes is unknown from this point of view, except some high-rise estate and industrial chimneys in the distance may give a clue. What the river will touch in that distance, is hidden from sight.

It is here, under the bridge, where along the river bank, just off the path, a man stares in the distance, seeing nothing. A young guy, probably somewhere in his early twenties, pushing his bicycle passes by.

'H'llo,' the friendly youngster says in a way most strangers would greet, if they'd ever greet.

'Hi,' the staring man replies in automatic fashion. He doesn't actually take any notice of the stranger with his bike.

The young man walks past him, not thinking for a second about the despair emanating from the staring man. Only when he's already twenty passes ahead, he turns around. 'Are you alright?'

No reply.

Probably someone who likes to keep to himself despite the miserable look in his eyes. Just let him be... but what if... no way, he's not going to jump... is he? 'Sir is everything okay?'

'Uh, what?'

'I said, is everything okay? I mean, uh,' how to say this? 'I mean, you look like you're having a tough day.' Having a tough day? How on earth could he say that. He should have better said: 'I couldn't help myself but notice that you seem troubled.'

'Tough day?' The older man disturbed from his stoic deep thinking, or whatever he was doing as he stared in the distance, looked up. He now glanced at the younger man with his bike. 'Tough day? The toughest I've ever been.'

'I'm sorry about that,' the young cyclist responds, still twenty passes away. 'Anything I can help?'

'Help? I've been waiting for help my whole life! Help. No one helped me then, no one can help me now.'

This doesn't seem promising. The younger guy became concerned. What is he getting himself into now?

'Uhm... Sorry about that. I thought... I just wanted to... uhm... make sure you wouldn't do anything stupid.' Anything stupid? Come on, man, you can do better than that!

'Stupid? Like jump? No mate, not today.' The older man paused, turned and looked back at the river. For the first time he noticed how fast it flowed under the bridge. Food wrappers and twigs floating in the water would pass the wide bridge in mere seconds. 'Although...,' he sighed.

BLARE!

A large truck crossed the bridge, and something must have upset the driver to honk his horn so loudly. Both men were startled and looked up.

The truck passed and only the normal sound of traffic across the bridge remained. If one listened carefully one could even hear the wind hustle through the trees.

'I'm sorry, uhm... I overreacted,' the older man said softly. His mouth curled a little as if he'd become shy. He didn't want to punish someone, definitely not the first person who'd cared to ask.

The young man walked up to the older one. He noticed the thinning black hair with streaks of silver. The man's overcoat was black and thinning, too, to the extent that small holes could be seen. Under his coat, the man wore a knitted brown, gray and army green scarf. His face was worn and showed wrinkles, in particular around the eyes. The eyebrows were bushy and black with longer gray hairs; he sported a couple of days' worth of gray stubble on his chin and cheeks.

The most important feature the young man couldn't help but notice were the older man's eyes. These gray-green eyes were filled with a sense of melancholy and helplessness. With these eyes, the man stared across the river, but he didn't seem to really look at anything. All he seemed to see was this void, this depth, this place in his mind he couldn't get away from.

'Uh… what did you mean with no one can help me now?' Still holding his bicycle with one hand, the young man paused and tried to choose his words better this time. 'To be honest, probably I can't help… uhm, but I can at least listen… uhm, if that is what you want of course, I mean, uhm, if you want to share anything and want me to listen.'

Choosing better words? It sounded more like rambling.

The older man lifted his shoulders a little as he took a deep breath in. He sighed. 'Well,' he said as he turned his head slightly towards to young stranger, 'I'm not sure you're up for this.'

He shrugged his shoulders again and lifted one hand out of his pocket to gesture for the young man to come closer. His eyes looked sternly, but he still showed a half smile. 'I'm certainly not asking you to stay, or listen, for that matter, to my load of rubbish,' he continued, 'but if you really want to, I certainly do appreciate that.'

'Well, okay.' The man put down his bicycle in the grass next to the path. He stepped closer next to the stranger he just met. Both men stood side by side, gazing over the water, staring across the river.

Both men were silent. All anyone could hear was the sound of the wind in the trees as the wind became stronger and turned, and the noise of traffic moving across the bridge as it grew fainter by the turning of the wind. For at least a few minutes, no one spoke.

The river didn't stop flowing. The wind kept growing stronger and blew even some dust and leaves in the river. The leaves were quickly picked up by the water and floated along with twigs, plastic bags and confectionary wrappers downstream. Golden and brown leaves were carried by the brown-looking river towards the high-rise buildings and industrial terrain. Will they ever reach that distant area, or will they even be taken to distant lands, or even the sea? Or will these dried leaves become water-logged and decay, sinking deep to the riverbed, never to be seen again?

As the young man let his eyes follow some of the leaves that were blown past them in front of them, he saw a glimpse of the older man's cheek. A tear rolled across this cheek.

The older man coughed and cleared his throat. 'I'm sorry.' He shuffled his feet in embarrassment as he continued, 'you really don't have to do this. I appreciate your concern, but it really isn't necessary.'

'It's okay. Even if I completely don't understand your situation, I can at least show interest in a fellow human being who's obviously doing it tough.' He smiled and looked straight at the older man.

The older man sighed. He cleared his throat again.

'Well…, the short version is, I ain't got nothing left. I had lots, just a couple of years ago, when I still used to work up there.' With his head he pointed across the river, towards the bridge. Obviously, that's where the city center is with its business district.

'Okay…, what happened?' The young man's voice broke just as he tried to ask that question. He straightaway tried to clear his throat to repeat the question, but the older man interrupted him.

'What happened? I lost everything. I lost my investments, my job, my family. Everything.'

'But how?'

The older man sighed deeply before he continued. His eyes became blank and two more tears started rolling down his cheeks.

'It started with these two investment projects. They were meant to change the world… I mean in a good way, they were meant to actually help people.' The man turned his head to look straight at his younger companion. He sighed again.

'I was never meant to lose all my money. When these people came and presented the projects – they were two separate ones – I was sure I could trust them. And they were trustworthy, they were in it for the right reasons.

'I had this money sitting there anyway, and I thought if I could do something good with it. Help people, make this world a better place, leave a better world for the next generation. You know what I mean?

'But it all went poof!' He raised his hands in the air and looked up to show and see that what he had, he'd now released to the wind. 'The two projects, one after the other, fell through. Not enough investment to carry on the first, but they'd already spent it on the property to shelter the homeless – it was a homeless food and shelter project. And the property prices dropped just as they had to sell, so they went bust and only those who are in it for their reputation got some money back. Everyone else, they lost it all.

'The second project, well, there was this corrupt accountant.' He shrugged his shoulders and sighed as he said, 'everyone thought he was trustworthy. After all he did the bookkeeping of this large church downtown. Of course, someone like that must be trustworthy. Well, no! He wasn't. We found out and that church found out soon after. They even had to sell their building to make ends meet after he'd gone with the wind.'

'What project was that,' the young man asked.

'Oh, it was to help build orphanages in Haiti and some other places in Central America. I can't really remember. It doesn't matter now anyway.'

'So, you lost everything, because of these projects?'

'Pretty much. I'd invested all my savings. My boss heard of this, and being his financial strategist, he was afraid I would do something dodgy with his money to make up for my loss, so he conveniently made me redundant with the first following round of reorganizations.'

'And your family?'

'My wife…' his voice broke. He paused as he swallowed. 'My wife died in a car crash two weeks after I'd lost my job. She died here, on that bridge.'

'Oh… uhm… I'm so s-sorry.'

'We were actually separated already, but you know, she was hoping we'd work something out… I was too stubborn and refused to talk to her right after the second project went up in thin air.'

Suddenly, the old man bent over and fell on his knees. He started crying with his head between his knees.

'I… I… I miss her now so much!' he sobbed. 'If I could only, if I could only tell her I'm sorry.'

The young man knelt beside him, but he wasn't sure what to do next. Moments passed, the wind died down and the noise of traffic on the bridge picked up again. They both were quiet. The old man sobbed in silence, the young man sighed and stared.

After a few minutes, the young man lifted his hand and gently, or some would say awkwardly, placed it on the sobbing man's shoulder. The man started crying louder.

'I'm so sorry about all this,' the young man said. 'I could not even imagine...' but he couldn't finish his sentence as he couldn't even imagine what to say next.

'Then I lost everything,' the crying man continued with shaky voice. His whole body shook. 'I had to sell everything to pay the bills, and to cover the funeral. No job, no family, no nothing.'

He paused, he quieted in his shaking. The wind started picking up again.

'Now all I have is this body and the clothes I'm wearing to cover it,' he continued. 'I even ain't got no food left.'

Wow. It just hit the young man. He really lost everything. What about himself, he still had everything: parents, a girlfriend, or actually 'fiancée' (he still had to get used to it even though it's been already for two months), a job and an apartment. How would that be to lose it all?

'Uh... actually,' he cleared his throat, 'I've got a couple of sandwiches in my backpack. Would you care?'

The older man lifted his head slightly and looked at the young man's friendly face. In between his tears a little smile briefly showed, but then amazement hit his eyes.

'I mean, I'm happy to give it to you,' he continued. 'I know it isn't much, but it's all I have on me right now.'

'Sure..., uh, thank you. Yes, please... Uh, I haven't eaten for days, just standing here.'

The young man reached for his backpack and opened the side compartment. He pulled out a packet wrapped in that thin paper sandwich places wrap their products in.

'It's freshly made an hour ago. I was meant to get it and share it with my girlfriend... uh... fiancée up in the park a mile from here. Got a flat tire just a mile back.'

The older man smiled. 'That, well, that explains why you're not on it. I mean, you were walking, not cycling.'

'Yeah,' I was actually pretty annoyed, 'but then, as I started walking, the breeze cleared my mind, and I just looked at the river. I thought, I wished I had a boat, so I could sail and still make it in time to the park.' He grinned as he said it.

'But, don't you have to go to your fiancée now?'

'Nah, it was just for her half-hour lunchbreak. I rang her and left a message

I wouldn't be able to make it in time. She wouldn't be able to wait for me. I hope she isn't worried about me, though.'

'Oh, okay. Well, I know this isn't what you wanted, but for whatever it's worth, I'm happy you got a flat tire. I mean, I'm happy you walked by.' The older man looked embarrassed as he said it.

'It's okay… For whatever it's worth, I'm happy I did too. My fiancée will be okay, too, when I tell her. She's very understanding. She'll actually be surprised, because normally she's the outgoing one, I'm more reserved.' He then looked at his sandwiches as he'd opened up the package. 'Well, you eat this. You must be starving.'

'Thank you, thank you very much,' the older man said as he took one of the sandwiches, 'but you eat too. I really like your company and I do have too much pride to sit here and eat alone. There's too much; I couldn't finish it all by myself.'

They both took a sandwich and ate. They looked across the river, staring in the distance.

'So, this river? Do you know where it ends up?'

The young man walks past him, not thinking for a second about the despair emanating from the staring man. Only when he's already twenty passes ahead, he turns around. 'Are you alright?'

W hen it comes to my personal thoughts in this story, I always look at what strikes to me, what stands out. Isn't it strange that two strangers can have a deep conversation early on? In our present culture, we often pass by so many faces, but do we actually notice any of them? Sometimes, we may see someone who stands out. The person with the weird jacket, for instance, or the colorful hat, or the more attractive person, or the one that hasn't seen a bath in a while.

To engage with a complete stranger and not have an agenda with it, no hidden (or plain) motive, that we don't often see. That is out of the ordinary to me. I'm pretty sure I don't easily walk up to someone and have a chat. But here, here we see a person taking interest in another just because there is the other, because the other may need someone with whom they can engage. Someone with whom they can share.

The second thing that hits me, that I'm definitely not good at, is that the young cyclist manages to see the good in a situation that seems to work against him. Of course, he probably had a hissy fit with his bike, or with whomever he thought he could blame. However, I'm pretty sure I'd have stayed in that negative situation for much longer. I'd have been so deep in my own negative thoughts, that I probably wouldn't have noticed the other person.

How easy we can be distracted from the people around us and their needs, just because we are so focused on our own situation, our own needs and our own insecurities. I'm catching myself with this, time and time again. When I, then, hear of other people doing it tough, I'm reminded of how little my situation compares to that of others. (Sometimes it's the other way around, but then I'm reminded to remain graceful to them, to not scoff at them or put them down for their ignorance. I can't go on this tangent, because this is a whole other topic!)

Sure, we all have our needs. We all need to survive. We all need to keep ourselves and our immediate world in check, so that we can also thrive. However, someone can have just eaten a few hours before and feel hungry (more like having an appetite, or to be 'peckish', as the British say), but it's completely different for someone who hasn't had food in days. They're starving!

Encouragement is like this. If we have lots of support around us, people that love us and are clear about this in their words and their actions, being encouraged by friends or family is like having something nice to eat without having to starve for it. It can become normal to us. Or maybe, we'd rather like to be encouraged with even greater thrill like winning an award or being publicly recognized.

However, if you feel like you're doing it all alone. You feel like the whole world is crumbling down, or, worse, fighting against you, while you're trying to keep up with it all. While you're trying to keep your head above the water. Encouragement is like a lifeline. It may be very simple, like a sandwich is a simple meal. The knowledge that someone out there cares, is worth a million! All of a sudden, you aren't alone. All of a sudden, you have someone that supports you, even if it's just a little.

This reminds me of myself in my early days at university. I had just moved out from home at the ripe old age of seventeen (I was an early student). I had left my family home in the Dutch countryside to live in Amsterdam. I wasn't not that well off and didn't have much myself. All my savings went to the bond for the place I'd found to live in.

I took some frozen meals, herbs, spices and cooking oil from home. The frozen meals would last me a few days and then I could buy some more ingredients and cook some for myself. However, when I went to the shop on my bike to buy some milk, bread and food to cook, I found that my card had declined. My first rent had come out and I wouldn't get my low-income study support until the next month.

I was devastated. I left the groceries at the checkout and cycled home. It was a depressing trip back to my place. It would've actually been a nice sunny ride if I'd only just been able to take some groceries home. I remember going through my stuff and managing to makeshift with some "meals" the next few days.

On the weekend, I would go back to my parents' place as most Dutch students do, to drop off their dirty laundry. My mom cooked some great food (probably my dad as well, but everyone only remembers their mother's or grandmother's cooking) and some of it I'd take back to Amsterdam as frozen meals.

There was this lady, she'd actually been one of my youth leaders growing up in church. She felt like she had to give me a bag to take with me to Amsterdam. The bag contained milk, bread, sardines and other food for cooking. The groceries I'd have to leave at the shop because I didn't have the money!

I know, I wasn't actually starving, as I still had something to eat. I could still restock at my parents and in the process have clean clothes! However, someone thought about me. And that they gave me what I really needed so that I wouldn't have to experience it all over again, that meant the world to me. It certainly impacted the way I viewed whatever had been entrusted to me: my finances, my studies, my family and friends. Just this simple bag of basic groceries.

This, again, reminds me of another story so many years ago. There was this little man, but not little in resources. He was quite wealthy. He was little in stature and easily overlooked. He'd made sure, however, that people wouldn't overlook him. He'd become the prime collaborator with foreign power that now occupied their land. He'd become a tax collector, and a corrupt one!

Then there was this important visitor, this famous man, who'd come into town. Knowing that he was too short to see over the crowd, and too hated by anyone that they wouldn't let him move to the front, he tried to find himself a way. He climbed up in a sycamore-fig tree. With low-hanging branches, it was perfect to climb in. With a thick cover of big leaves, it was perfect as a hideout. Here he would wait and see.

The crowd came closer and the important visitor came in sight. The visitor walked past surrounded by the masses, but then, he stopped. He stoped right next to the sycamore-fig tree. The tree the little man was in! The visitor looked up in between the branches through the leafy cover.

'Come down immediately,' the visitor shouted, 'I'm going to your place today.'

As remarkable it may sound to us, someone inviting themselves over for dinner (how obnoxious!), more so it was remarkable to the crowd's ears. Not that he'd invited himself over, they were quite used to providing hospitality to strangers. As a matter of fact, it was an honor if a visitor would pick your place!

The disgrace wasn't him inviting himself over, it was the place he'd picked. He'd picked the one place in town to which any good person wouldn't come close, unless they had to pay their taxes, of course. He'd picked the tax collector's house, the collaborator's house, the corrupt and scandalous place!

The effect? The little man came down straight away. He felt so honored, so validated as a person (we really can't imagine how important it was for these people to have guests!), so encouraged, he changed his behavior on the spot. He decided to quit his corrupt business and to reimburse everyone he'd mistreated in the past, with interest. The little man's name? Zacchaeus of Jericho[1].

Just a little stop to take interest in someone, and to share a few words of value. This is encouragement. We don't know what it will carry with it, or where it goes, but we do know where it can come from. Just as the river has a source and an outlet into the sea, encouragement can flow from us to another person to the next till it touches and impacts many.

Let's be people who stop to notice others. Who think about other people's needs. Let's be people who share those few words or provide a listening ear. Who bring simple encouragement like a simple sandwich to the hungry. Maybe we extend someone a lifeline. Maybe we may save someone from starvation. Maybe someone else will do the same to us when we find ourselves in need.

> As a river flowing beyond mountains,
> Far over the horizon it flows.
> No one knows where its water goes,
> what it touches or where it comes close.
>
> Encouragement can move mountains,
> Mountains of desperation and need.
> Who would know its effect or its deed?
> Who'd know the hungry it'll feed?

"Like apples of gold in settings of silver is a word spoken in right circumstances."
Proverbs 25:11, NASB.

UNEXPECTED

Lifting Weight

"It is one of the most beautiful compensations of this life that no man can sincerely try to help another without helping himself."
Ralph Waldo Emerson, *"Compensation"*, Essays: First Series

Unexpected. Encouragement is like a bench in a local gym. There was nothing special about this bench, just a typical gym bench. It had two legs that hit the ground with a wide base. Its top was nicely cushioned overlain with artificial leather. Its color was black: black legs, black top.

Whether it was old or quite new, no one could tell, except for the gym manager of course. It was well worn, patched up on the sides with thick tape, however, the artificial leather showed some more cracks around the corners. The black spray paint started to flake off from the metal legs exposing some bare steel. One thing was sure, it was well used.

Since the bench was not mounted to the floor, it was moved around quite a lot. People would place it under the *Smith machine* to use it for supported bench press exercises, or in stand-alone fashion for dumbbell press exercises, or worse, for triceps dips where shoes rip into its already-worn skin. Don't worry if you don't know these exercises. Many a person that works out, doesn't always know how to do these properly either. What is certain, its use was varied.

The bench had seen all the corners of the gym. It'd also felt most sweaty backs of the gym membership community. Every person coming to that gym for a workout, quick or long, knew this bench. Most people were happy to use it. Now, it was last left in the corner with the free weights where mirrors cover the walls.

One of the gym members was a on older gentleman. As the membership community was of a variety of ages from 18 years and up, this gentleman didn't really stand out. He'd be there most of the week, just after lunchtime. Specifically, he would come in for his hour-long workout on Mondays, Tuesdays, Wednesdays and Fridays. Thursday was his rest day as he'd catch up for lunch with some of his friends.

He usually kept to himself. Only the gym manager and a few of the regulars would have a brief chat with him in between exercises. Those who spoke with him, knew only a little about him. He'd only talk about his exercise routine, what he had for lunch and breakfast, and what was on TV the night before.

His friends, however, knew him through and through. They knew from one word whether he was up or down. They knew what he liked, and more importantly, what he disliked. What would make him happy, they knew, and what would set him off in anger, *they knew*. Every Thursday they'd meet for lunch. This had been the case ever since 1971 when they'd returned from service in Vietnam.

As it was Friday right after lunch, this older gym member arrived at the gym again for his last workout of the week. Normally friendly but reserved, this time his face looked grim. Normally he would say at least 'Good afternoon', or 'Hi there', but this time he didn't even acknowledge the gym assistant upon entry. As the assistant was busy working through indexing some invoices, she actually didn't notice or seem to care.

The man scanned his membership tag. A light turned green and a three-spike rotating gate, like those at the entry to an amusement park, was released. The man walked through the gate. He walked right up to the pigeonholes available for gym bag storage where he left his backpack. He pulled a towel and a water bottle from his bag as well as a little pocket notebook with a special compartment to store a pencil or a pen. He checked whether his pen was still tucked in as sometimes it'd fallen out and dropped to the bottom of his bag.

He didn't need to go to the change room as he'd already come wearing his exercise gear. He wore white runners with lots of dirt marks they were his general walking shoes, too. White socks pulled up to right under his knees were tucked in these shoes. Navy-blue shorts he sported with on top a gray polo shirt with diagonally running, fading black stripes. He was one of the very few gym members to also wear a once-white sweatband around his head, more to mask his receding hairline than to soak up any sweat.

Placing his notebook in the pocket of his polo shirt and taking his bottle and towel with him, he walked up to the water tap and filled his bottle. Once filled right to the brim – actually a few drops ran over wetting his hand – he walked to the exercise bikes. Every time he was at the gym, he'd start his workout with a ten-minute warmup cycling session.

This time it took the man a bit more effort to climb on the bike. Normally, his right knee was not making it too easy on him, but this time it was more painful and sensitive. He bit his lower lip and plowed through. His knee had never stopped him before, now it wouldn't stop him either. As a matter of fact, ever since he'd been coming to the gym regularly, his knee and the *remainder* of his right leg wasn't bothering him as much.

The cycling session was much harder this time. His leg really wasn't cooperating at all. The first cycle of his peddles was close to excruciating, but soon the pain would subside as his legs warmed up, but still it wasn't as smooth as usual – not that "smooth" is the right word to describe the usual either.

Smooth, what *could* one describe as smooth? A greased surface, or an oiled machine? What about peanut butter on a sandwich, or a really fine potato mash? But definitely not his life, especially over the past few days.

He grunted as he tried to get off the bike. *No smooth ride today, no smooth ride ever!* He looked around him, but no one seemed to notice. Good. At least something was still smooth: his ability to keep his cool.

He took out his pocket notebook and opened it to this week's notes. What did he do last, and what did he have to do this time? Great. He had to do lunges. Lunges, the exercise where with one leg you step forward and then lower yourself on bended knee. It's like kneeling down on one knee before royalty like a mighty king, or probably better, a princess whose hand you'd ask in marriage.

Well, lunges were going to be a bit of a problem today with his stubborn knee. So, it would probably be best if he'd do supported ones with one hand holding onto a bench. Okay, he'd then better find himself a bench.

A bench, a bench, where was there a bench? The older gentleman looked around, but he couldn't see any bench that was available. He walked further to look around at the other side where the free weights section was located. As he moved closer to that section, he noticed the big glass mirrors covering the walls in this part of the gym. He saw his own reflection from two angles as the mirrors covered two walls meeting in a corner. He noticed a slight limp in his right leg. He grunted.

But then, from the corner of his eye he saw a bench. He walked straight up to it, put his bottle and towel down and tried to get himself ready for his first set of lunges. How many he could do today? Probably not as many as last time, but that wouldn't matter, as long as he would do some just to keep himself fit.

Straightening his back, he took a deep breath. He closed his eyes and slowly released the air from his lungs. He repeated this twice more. After the third, again he took a deep breath just to start the exercise. He stepped out with his right leg and slowly, very slowly lowered himself...

'Excuses me.'

The words seemingly coming from nowhere (but actually they came from his left) startled him. He opened his eyes, staring straight in his own eyes in the mirror in front of him. He was not alone, someone was standing to his left. He pushed his right leg back next to his left. *Ouch!*

'Excuse me, sir,' the voice repeated. It was a female's voice, higher pitched than any men's voice he'd heard before. By the sounds of it, the woman wasn't that old, but generally he wasn't really good at guessing anyone's age based on their voice.

'Sorry, can I help you,' the older man replied while trying to suppress his pain. He swallowed and turned to his left. The woman, probably in her thirties (but he couldn't be sure) and with her hair tied up in a bun, looked at him with a questioning stern look.

'Uhm, yeah, this bench was taken.' She took a breath and swallowed. 'I'm sorry, I don't want to sound harsh, but I was actually using this bench.'

'Oh, really?' The older man couldn't believe it. He looked down to look at the bench. He now saw there was a gym bag and bottle placed at its end. 'Oh, I'm so sorry, I didn't notice your bag...'

'It's okay,' the woman replied. 'I'm sorry for my reaction. So often guys just push in and... uhm... I thought you were just like that.'

'Oh, no, I'm sorry. I should've paid better attention. My mind's been off lately.'

He paused and looked at his feet. They both smiled, but of course he didn't notice. He'd better go somewhere else to do his lunges. Where could there be another bench? He was about to turn around and pick up his stuff to go...

'Excuse me, sir.' Same voice, same words, but this time the tone was friendlier. 'Excuse me, before you go may I ask you something?'

'Sure.' He looked up and for the first time looked her in the eyes. They were deep brown in color with large pupils. Her eyelashes were long and thick, but that could also be because of mascara.

'Uhm, could you help me. I mean, I'm doing dumbbell bench presses and …uhm… I need someone to spot me.'

He now noticed the two dumbbells in her hands. They looked like 40 pounds each. Wow, she must be quite fit.

'Would you mind spotting me?' She repeated her question.

'Yes, uh… no, I mean. I can help, I mean,' he stumbled over his words. No one had ever asked him that. Not since Vietnam.

'Alright, thanks,' she said as she sat down at the end of the bench closest to the mirrored wall. She placed both dumbbells on her knees, one on her left knee and one on her right. The man placed his notebook, towel and bottle on the floor and stood over at the other end of the bench.

The woman lowered her upper body backwards as she lay down. She held the dumbbells in front of her, right up against her body. She took a deep breath in, and with a large burst and a grunt, she both emptied out her lungs and straightened her arms to lift the dumbbells right above her chest. She repeated this a few times.

Meanwhile, the man slightly bent stood behind her and kept his eyes on the moving dumbbells. He was still amazed at this woman's strength. Years ago, he could easily do 40 or 50 pounds, but now, this seemed like a fleeted echo from a distant past.

As the woman became fatigued in her arms, she struggled with the last few reps. The man grunted as he bent forward – still that right knee – and held his hands under her arms. He pulled her arms up as she pushed the dumbbells up. Both grunted.

After a couple of reps this way, the woman pulled the dumbbells to her body again and lifted herself into a seated position. Once up, she lowered the dumbbells down on the ground.

The men lifted himself up, too, and straightened up. Ouch! A sharp pain ran through his knee up his leg to his lower back. A tingling sensation ran through his lower body. He couldn't help himself, he moaned in pain.

'Are you okay?' The woman looked worried. 'Come, sit down on the bench.'

The man sat down, but again a sharp pain shot up.

'Is everything okay?' the woman asked again.

The man took a few deep breaths. He focused on what was in front of him, but he didn't actually notice the big man pushing a shoulder press machine who was in his line of sight. He just stared in the distance as he was moving his focus away from the pain. Slowly the stinging pain and the tingling in his lower body subsided.

'I'm okay,' he whispered. He gathered his strength and spoke a bit louder: 'I'm okay now.'

'You're sure?' the woman asked. 'You looked like you were in a lot of pain. I'm sorry that I asked you.'

'It's okay,' the older man replied. 'It's just my knee. It's been bothering me now for over four decades.'

As he spoke, he lowered the sock of his right leg.

'You see, below the knee, it's gone. It's all fake.' He pointed at his prosthetic that was attached to his knee. 'This one's only a few years old and is much better than what I had before, but still, my knee and leg have never felt the same since that dreadful day.'

'What happened?' she couldn't help but ask.

'What happened? A grenade, that's what happened. In Vietnam in 1971, that's what happened.'

'Oh, I'm sorry to hear that. I didn't mean to... uhm...' She paused as she didn't know what to say about it all.

'It's okay,' the old man smiled. He took a breath and sighed. 'It actually feels good to talk to someone else about this for once. I mean, only my friends and the veterans services know about this. With no one else, I bothered sharing it.'

'Great,' the woman said with sarcasm. 'First, I yell at you. Then, when you're obviously in pain, I ask you to help me and make it even worse. To top it all, I continue by poking in your private life, something you don't share with others! I'm really sorry about all this.'

'It's okay.' The man felt he was repeating this sentence a few times now. 'After the past few days, I could do with a chat to someone. To be honest, I actually felt flattered when you asked me to spot for you. No-one's asked me to help them for a while.'

They both smiled as they sat on the bench.

Then the man's face turned grim. He sighed. After a brief pause, he continued: 'No-one's asked for my help since that dreadful day.'

'You mean the day you were hit by a grenade, weren't you?'

'Yeah,' the man sighed. A tear rolled over his left cheek. 'That day, I lost my leg, but worse, I also lost a very good friend.'

'I'm so sorry to hear that. It must've been terrible, the war and all.'

'Terrible? Nah, that word isn't good enough to describe the horrors we've seen and experienced.' Again, the man paused. He took a deep breath, and as he let the air escape from his lungs, he said: 'My friend Larry... he was a good man. Despite the horrors, he stayed a good man. He didn't hold grudges, not even against the enemy. He was also a good friend who'd give it all for his friends.' He paused again. 'Well, he gave it all.'

'You mean, he gave his life... for... for you?'

'Yes, he did. The grenade, it was ours, was a dud. We were in our camp, not even close to enemy lines. Larry saw the thing drop to the ground, from where I can't remember, but as it dropped the pin fell out, or was pulled out.' Tears then started flowing. 'He flung me to the side... and he tried to throw it away, or cover it with his body... it went so fast...'

The man let his head sink in his hands. The woman sat stunned beside him. Finally, she put out one hand and put it on the man's shoulder, the shoulder closest to her. The man sobbed.

'And now, Johnny is dying too.'

The last words caught the woman by surprise. 'Johnny?' she asked, before she could hold herself in.

'Johnny,' the man said with a trembling voice. 'He was the one who pulled me from that ravage. He's got cancer. He told me yesterday.'

The man sobbed again. The woman could not utter anything but whispered: 'I'm so sorry. I'm so sorry.'

They sat there like that for about five minutes, although to them it probably seemed half an hour, at least.

Once the man gained control of himself again, he straightened himself up and placed his hands beside him resting on the bench. He snorted. 'I'm sorry to bother you with this,' he said. 'I shouldn't do this to you. What've you got to do with an old wreck like me?'

'Don't say that. I'm happy to listen to your story, to be there for you. You're sure you haven't shared any of this with anyone else?'

The man looked down at his shoes. One had his real foot and the other just some metal and some polymeric material. 'No, other than my friends from

Vietnam, no-one.'

'Then I feel honored. It's an honor to listen to you, and it's an honor to meet one of our country's heroes.'

The man smiled. This was the first time in a long while he'd heard someone call him a hero. Larry was the hero, Johnny was a hero – but *him*?

'Thank you.' He looked her in her deep brown eyes, they twinkled. 'Thank you.'

He stood up and turned his head one more time towards her. She was still sitting on the bench, the bench that had started this conversation.

'Thank you, ma'am. The honor was mine.'

After bidding her a good day, he wandered off. With his towel and bottle in his hands, he walked towards the pigeon hole where he'd kept his bag. As he made his way out of the gym, he couldn't help it but notice that he felt lighter in his step. Somehow, his knee didn't bother him as much as it had done earlier. He also felt lighter in his heart, somehow as he'd opened up, he'd let a weight lift off him.

Suddenly, as a rush one thought popped in his mind. He touched his pocket in his polo shirt. 'Darn.' His pocket notebook wasn't there. *Well, then we'll probably see each other again*, he thought as he continued his step.

Looking at this story, I can't escape the question: who's supporting whom? Was the man supporting the woman in her workout, or was the woman supporting the man with his pain? Or were they both relying on each other's support?

Support. It's such a small word, but its meaning is immense. The Oxford Dictionary gives a variety of definitions depending on its use, whether as a verb or a noun. Two that stand out and, are related, are "approval, encouragement, or comfort" and "source of comfort or encouragement". Support *is* encouragement and *a source of* encouragement.

Support comes from the Latin word *supportare,* which in itself is a combination of the words *sub-* (from below) and *portare* (to carry). To carry from below, that is the original meaning of support. We can encourage people by carrying them from below.

Of course, we don't have to physically lift them up or carry the weight for them. We aren't all at the gym spotting for one another and helping each other lifting heavy weights. However, life is like a massive gym workout where challenges and difficulties train, or stretch (which feels more like it), our ability to cope, our resilience.

The first meaning in the Oxford Dictionary for support as a noun is "bear all or part of the weight of; hold up". Encouragement can do this. Encouragement can come in someone's struggles and let them know, *you're not in it alone. Let's bear this weight together. Let's hold it up.*

Struggles, difficulties, experiences of utter sadness and grief can weigh us down. We often wish someone could come in and understand our struggle and just ease the weight of it. Supporting encouragement isn't always about understanding the gravity of a situation. Often, the person stepping in to

They both smiled as they sat on the bench.
Then the man's face turned grim. He sighed. After a brief pause, he continued: 'No-
one's asked for my help since that dreadful day.'

support doesn't understand, but their support can certainly help ease the weight. It may even provide us with the final strength to overcome the battle we face.

I know another story about that. It is a story about an old man somewhere in his eighties. Despite his age he had the immense, or rather impossible, task to lead a large group of people. He acted as their chief advisor, judge and lawgiver.

He didn't just oversee his family, or extended family if you will; not even his clan. He led his own tribe. To top it, he led eleven more tribes, a whole nation! He led them from the place where they were mistreated and misjudged to their homeland, the land they'd left four hundred years earlier and would now return to.

Other than his own people, not many other tribes or nations liked their plans of returning home. Some would try to deny their claim, others would deny entry to cross their land. Even his own people were grumbling all the time and rather put up with the second or third-rank status they had and all the abuse and slave labor that accompanied it.

There was this one tribe, or nation (the boundaries between those at that time were quite blurred), that actually couldn't care less whether he and his people would make it or not. They were not interested in their success or their failure. All they were interested in were their possessions: their gold and silver, their life stock, their clothes and tapestry. If they wouldn't hand it to them freely, they'd take it by force.

The old man and his people were attacked by this gruesome people group. As coward raiders usually do, they attacked the weak and the young first; they raided the rear[1]. The old man sent his second-in-charge to gather all fighting men and fight off this army of raiders.

The peculiar part of this story is that the old man overseeing the battle had to raise his arms so that his men could win. As soon as he'd drop them, his people were losing. As you can imagine, an old man can only keep his arms up for so long. He can't do it all day. Have you tried it recently? Let's do it right now… I see you get the point.

Since the raiders came in large numbers – think of it, no one would attack a large crowd with only a handful – the defending army had to fight for a long time. The old man's arms eventually grew weary and they'd drop.

Here comes the greatest part of the story: the old man wasn't alone! He'd brought with him two men. One was his older brother and the other a man less well-known but most likely a major leader close in age. Aaron and Hur were their names. They'd come along with the sole purpose to support the old man in his incredible task.

What one old man could impossibly do by himself, all of a sudden became possible with the help of two more old men. As soon as the old leader was about to drop his hands, they sat him down on a stone and together held up his hands. Now it was much easier, still not comfortable I think, but at least bearable.

It was through the support of these two men that the old man could accomplish his task, so that his people, the Israelites, could gain the victory. The raiders from Amalek were defeated and fled. Many people's lives were saved because two old men decided to support another old man. This old man's name was Moses[2].

The power of support, of help bearing the weight and upholding someone in the face of adversity, is immense and shouldn't be underestimated. It should move us to want to provide support to others.

Firstly, we can and should provide a support network for those in our families that have their struggles or are trying to find their way in life[3]. This doesn't mean we do the work for them. It means we let them know that we're there for them, that they have a safe place with us where they can unload their stress, anxiety, or conflicting emotions.

Secondly, it also means that we are there to listen to them as they weigh up options when a new opportunity arises. Support is not only meant for those who are doing it tough. It is also essential for helping others reach their full potential.

Support is like the surface of the Earth. It keeps us grounded right where we are, we don't sink through it (unless you're on quicksand). When we're trying to move forward regardless of the situation, with our feet we push ourselves off the ground. The ground pushes back, it supports our feet, so that we can move forward. From the same surface plants grow as they "push themselves upward" against the ground. The Earth's surface supports us all.

The same way we can provide support to those around us. Let's help them push themselves off the ground, so they can thrive. Let's not push them into the ground or let them sink into quicksand and drown.

Of course, support can only be effective if the person needing it accepts it. Accepting support is a form of humility. You need to set aside your pride of wanting to do it alone. You need to come to the conclusion that you need help or, at least, someone to motivate you and spur you on.

This last comment, I certainly take to heart myself. If you'd ask my family, I'm quite a prideful person. As a teenager some would have called me arrogant. My parents sighed so many times when I tried to have the last say in any arguments we had. Personally, I would excuse myself as being tenacious. I don't easily like to give in or give up. But now I admit, pride is one of my areas of weakness (ask me again in one of my prideful moments and I may disagree).

One practical example in which my pride tripped me up (discounting the countless times I caused fights and disagreements) is when I hit the gym as a late teen. I liked working out and I still do. What I didn't like, which may surprise you after reading the story before, is asking for help or someone to spot me.

One moment I tried bench pressing. The first sets went alright, so I increased the load. Being inexperienced I didn't factor in that my muscles were getting quite fatigued, so I loaded more than I could lift one rep or more (a rep, or repetition, is a single movement within a set of an exercise). Lying on the bench, face and chest upward, feet on the ground, I lifted the barbell once up and down toward my chest. Then I tried lifting it up again and… I couldn't. My muscles caved in; they'd given up. I was stuck.

It was a good thing that I wasn't alone in that space. A couple of big guys, obviously more experienced than I, came to my rescue. They helped me up from under the barbell and straightaway offered me support to spot for me when I needed. I thanked them, but after that incident went straight out to the locker room. I felt humiliated, but actually I was hurt in my pride.

To be people of encouragement we should be able to both provide and receive support. In a sense we should just be like that extensively used bench at the start of the story. It supported anyone in their exercises, and it was moveable; it let itself be carried to different places in that gym so that it could fulfill its purpose. The biggest support to both the man and the woman in our story was that bench.

To uphold, to carry the weight,
To bear the load, crooked or straight.
Support is essential, a saving force.
It helps us grow, the encouragement source.
Supportare, to carry from below,
To extend and accept, for us to bestow.

"A friend loves at all times, and a brother is born for a time of adversity.'
Proverbs 17:17, NIV.

Hidden Treasure

"Those who dream by day are cognizant of many things which escape those who dream only by night."
Edgar Allan Poe, *Complete Tales and Poems*

Unexpected. Encouragement is like a flower, or rather a bed of flowers. A bed of flowers blossoming during the day but planted at night. It was made of a colorful sea of pink, white and orange daisies, pink and white azaleas and white and yellow camellias. Interspersed in between these flowers and around grew blue and pink forget-me-not plants.

The flowerbed was graciously planted in front of a bougainvillea bush so that the floral splash appeared against a backdrop of dark green and burgundy foliage filled with amaranth flowers. Anyone walking past this garden, couldn't help but stop to notice and take in the colorful display so thoughtfully created and presented. Even if the colors wouldn't stop anyone in their pace, it would be the air taking up a whiff of the aroma spread by this garden that didn't only contain this flower bed, but bushes of many more varieties both native and exotic.

In addition, the garden was filled with pleasant fauna most of the year. In summer the garden was filled with many colorful butterflies and, as long as flowers bloomed, birds would fly in to drink the nectar or bathe in the little birdbath at the center of the garden.

No one walking past and seeing this display of natural, but cultivated, wonder would ever believe that this garden was located in the nation's ugliest town. Actually, most gardens in this town showed a beautiful display in harmony with the houses they harbor. Some were simpler than others, some showed greater workmanship than others. However, all of them exhibited a warm sort of beauty prepared by a hand of loving care.

Beautiful gardens in the nation's ugliest town? How could that be? Which town could it be, anyway?

It's the town of Moleovale, located where grasslands and sparse forests meet the desert. Seated in a valley through which a seasonal river meanders: the Moleo. The river, rather a creek, tends to flood during the wet autumn and winter months, but is completely dry in summer. Traditionally the grasslands have been used as pastures for grazing cattle and sheep. The forested areas provided lumber for local buildings and fences, but in general the wood of the Moleo pine is not that good so a strong lumber industry never developed.

With the arrival of the new interstate freeway in the 1970s, suddenly the town became a hub of refreshment along a long empty stretch of road. "Moleovale, the last stop before the desert starts!" was its motto. A booming business started up of motels, service stations and mechanics, as well as supermarkets and local tourist shops selling miniature sheep.

Being largely developed in the 1970s, the town was designed based on the architecture and urban needs of the time. The roads were wide and based on a grid of perfectly north-south and east-west running streets. Every house was detached, and no apartment blocks were ever built.

The houses, however, were all quite different. Some resembled more closely a modern minimalist look with lots of square forms and concrete walls, others exhibited a more late-art-deco style with a variety of straight lines and curves and decorative features typical of late 1930s and 1940s architecture elsewhere. Two houses were built in a colonial style. Despite the wide range of styles uncommon for the 1970s, they were all designed by one architect: Leo von Eckdorf.

Leo von Eckdorf was regarded the town's father of style. He invented the way Maleovale should look and how it was developed. There still is a statue of him right in front of the local town hall holding a pencil and a ruler. "He measured Maleovale, he created Maleovale" the titular reads.

Unfortunately, Leo never was able to see how his creation would look like. In early 1973, when only half the town had been developed, he died of a heart attack. The father of style of Maleovale only saw the road grid with buildings interspersed over the full area Maleovale still covers today. The town hall with his statue in front was only completed in 1979.

As the town developed, the initial parts were still according to Von Eckdorf's plans, and in honor of his work they also kept the town hall according to his initial design. During this period many journalists and writers heralded the town for its looks. "Beauty and elegance combined with practicality and purity" as one New York Times' reporter once put it.

However, since his death, the town planning services changed the design and the location of many buildings. They were appalled by the experimental nature of the architecture and made it more recognizable to the common man, woman and child. At least, so they thought.

Many decorative features were omitted, and garden spaces were either turned into mulched areas with one tree or a simple lawn with a blackberry bush. These spaces required minimal care: just a trim and a mow. Contrasts between buildings were diminished and similarly styled houses were placed together in the same area.

Concrete was seen as the cheap solution to the originally sandstone Von Eckdorf liked to use. Pathways and sidewalks were concreted, parkland was increasingly concreted, all for the sake of practicality (and savings on any municipal maintenance workers). Even the Town Hall Plaza, the garden square of Von Eckdorf in front of the town hall was completely concreted to function as a parking lot. Von Eckdorf's statue stands sadly in this concrete wasteland.

With the arrival of graffiti tags on many walls (the kind local gangs use to mark their territory) and the disregard of cleanliness of the public space, the town slowly fell into disarray. The concrete cracked and crumbled under the harsh conditions desert areas often experience. Even Von Eckdorf's writing hand had once fallen off; the mended crack is still clearly visible.

It wasn't before long, Maleovale was nicknamed Malignedville. Despite its continuing industry in hospitality and car services to travelers on the interstate, the rest of the town lost its flare and its spirit. In a 1980s report Maleovale was described an "eyesore", in the 1990s "a hub for the distasteful", and in the 2000s it was said "Von Eckdorf's failed experiment never to be repeated". For twenty consecutive years it had been elected the nation's ugliest town.

However, something changed three years ago. Trees started to appear more alive. Lawns started to look neater and fuller. Flowers started to grow in different areas across town. Slowly, night by night, people's gardens experienced makeovers. The Maleovale Gazette called it the "Maleovale Miracle".

People were wondering where this change in the town's looks had come from. They asked the two municipal maintenance people still employed, but even they couldn't tell. They certainly didn't have the budget nor the expertise to make such a thing happen. Even the mayor couldn't provide a satisfying answer.

The town was bustling with rumors and stories. They called the mystery landscaper and maintenance worker the Flower Man, the Tree Trimmer, the Maleovalescaper or the Night Gardener. Children in town had their own stories about him and called him the Secret Santa.

Every week the Maleovale Gazette would dedicate a separate page on how different gardens had been transformed or improved. They'd also publish columns of two local expert on the mystery person, who'd summarize the latest rumors about his looks and whereabouts, as well as his motives.

Apparently, he'd clad himself in black, sabotage streetlights and cover gardens under black tarps. After he'd finished, he would fix the streetlights and remove the tarp. Others were not convinced by such stories of extreme laborious endeavors. They rather thought of him as actually being invisible. The children believed that Secret Santa would ride a sleigh across the night sky and spread his miracle dust that would make the world look better. After all, during Christmas everything looked better and more beautiful, too.

Some were less trusting or gullible. They actually thought the local newspaper was behind it all to create news in an otherwise dull town. After all, before this mystery person started stuffing around people's gardens, the editor was about to fire half his staff. Now she doubled her staff due to a tripling in sales. However, only a few would go as far as to openly accuse the Gazette, and if anyone ever wrote an open letter, the newspaper never published it.

Eric and Anita Bloome lived in this town with its failed design but its mystery gardens. They weren't there often as they both worked in a large city a four-hours' drive away. They would only come home for holidays and long weekends. They'd bought their home just to live in a quiet and affordable place as well as close to desert and sandstone cliffs. They both loved rock climbing and hiking under extreme circumstances. In addition, Anita's parents had recently moved to Maleovale, too.

In the city Eric worked as a structural engineer in a large engineering company. They were charged to look at the design and construction of the new metropolitan railway tunnel connecting east with west. Being only in his mid-thirties he had risen through the ranks substantially, managing a whole team of civil, environmental and structural engineers.

Anita worked as a successful lawyer for an esteemed law firm. She would represent corporations and firms and advise them on how to conduct or avoid hostile takeovers. Between Eric and her, she made the most money and she received invitations to functions which made them move among the upper circles of the city's elite. She was only a little older than Eric.

Because they were away from home so often, and the Maleovale Gazette's second favorite topic was on the recent crimewave, Eric decided they'd need a security system installed including cameras and spotlights. These would usually do the trick of scaring off potential burglars, at least so he thought.

The next long weekend, they'd come home again. After a month of long days, overtime and many civil obligations, they were looking forward to a few days of rest, sitting on the sofa drinking red wine and of course one day of hiking in the desert.

As they were discussing their plans for the night, what to eat and what movie to watch, Anita's mouth suddenly dropped wide open. She let out a high-pitched scream. Eric, being usually a bit slower in his response, firstly wondered about Anita's reaction, but soon after he couldn't muffle a shout of his own.

'What the...?'

'How on earth,' Anita interrupted. 'How did that happen?'

As the car had turned into their driveway, both were gazing at their wide-open garage. They were sure they'd left it closed. How could it be open before they'd come home? Or more worrying, who did this and why?

Eric parked the car in the driveway and ran out of the vehicle. As he was about to run into the house, Anita's experience in law kicked in.

'Eric don't go in,' she shouted. 'If it's a break-in we'd better get the cops in first.' Even though she was a corporate lawyer, she still remembered the basics of criminal law and crime scene reporting.

Eric came to a halt right in front of the opened garage. He looked in, but he couldn't see much in the dark. As his eyes slowly adjusted, he could make out shapes. There was the lawn mower in the corner. There was his mountain bike. His workshop area seemed all right; from the distance it didn't seem anyone had disturbed it. When it comes to his tools, he sure is a neat freak, so he'd notice it from a mile away if anyone had rummaged through it or had misplaced something. As far as he could tell, *the garage was the way they'd left it.*

'How's it looking?' Anita asked as she walked right up to him. 'Does it look like anything's missing?'

'Nope, it all looks like the way I usually keep the garage. Maybe, they'd come out this way, but the door to the house itself is closed.' Eric pointed at the door in the back of the garage through which they'd normally enter the house after parking the car.

'Let's check the front door, maybe there's evidence of a break-in?' Anita suggested as she shrugged her shoulders.

Eric had one last look at the garage and the opened roller door. No damage, no evidence of any forced entry. In a late response he moved his lips as to say 'sure', but no sound came out. He was too deep in thought. Even if he'd said something, Anita didn't hear it as she'd already walked up to their front door.

Anita examined the front door and shook the door handle and the lock. The door was closed; it wouldn't open. It was still locked. She took her keys out of her handbag and unlocked the door. No signs of anyone that would have forced their way in this way. As she opened the door, she felt a cold breeze of air coming from inside the house. The airflow made her back shiver. As she opened the door wider, the door screaked a little. She stared in a dark, cool space. She slowly bent forward to look in as a hand grabbed her shoulder. Anita screamed.

'Don't worry, it's just me,' said Eric's voice with a chuckle. 'I was right behind you.'

'Don't you ever scare me again like that,' Anita yelled angry and flustered at the same time. 'This is serious, someone may actually still be in our house, and mister tries to scare his wife.'

'I didn't try… but now you say it… ah, never mind.'

They both walked into the house carefully not to touch anything. As their eyes adjusted to the lower light, all curtains had been drawn, they looked at their place. Everything seemed in order. There was no sign of someone looking through their cupboards and drawers. The TV was still in its place, the artwork hadn't been taken off the walls either. Puzzled, they looked everywhere, but they couldn't find an answer to the mystery of the opened garage door.

After looking everywhere, they reconvened in the kitchen for a quick drink.

All the rooms in the house were exactly the way they'd left it. Why then was the garage door open? After both taking a glass of water, Eric leaned backward on the kitchen bench. Anita was about to ask whether they'd still get the police involved, she turned her eyes to Eric and gasped.

'What's the matter,' Eric said with clear surprise in his eyes.

'The flowers, the vase. We didn't leave them here.'

'You're sure? You usually like flowers…'

'No, no,' Anita interrupted, 'I do, but I didn't leave these here. They'd have withered, but these are fresh!'

Eric turned around to look at a water-filled vase keeping a bunch of white and orange daisies, pink and white azaleas and white and yellow camellias. They certainly looked fresh, and they certainly looked bright.

'These are beautiful,' Anita continued. 'They're so simple, but also so beautiful.'

'There's a note in it.' Eric was always a bit more to the point. He wasn't really the romantic one in their relationship.

'Welcome home. Found these in your garden and thought you'd like them. Mum and dad.' Anita read out loud from the little folded note.

'It was your mum and dad!' Eric shouted, but Anita looked wary as if she didn't understand. 'I mean, your mum and dad left the flowers here and must've left the garage door open. Not sure why, but it makes sense.'

'Did you leave them with keys to the garage then?'

'Yeah, of course. Sometimes your dad needs the lawn mower. It's not fair to let him wait till we're back in town again. It's his anyway.'

'Okay…,' Anita still wasn't too sure, but Eric's explanation seemed plausible. Nonetheless, as a lawyer she just couldn't live with not knowing the full story. 'How about ringing them, just to make sure?'

They rang her parents. As it turned out, her dad had come by and took the lawn mower from the garage. As Eric explained, the lawn mower was his anyway, they only kept it at the Bloomes' house, because of lack of space. That morning, he'd returned it, but in his forgetfulness, must've forgotten about closing the garage. The flowers he'd taken from the garden.

'You must've been visited by the Flower Man. You usually don't keep your flowers that neat.'

'Thanks dad, but what're you talking about? Who's this Flower Man, or what you call him?'

'The Flower Man! The Malaeovalescaper, the mystery man making all the gardens look like they were in Eden. You're sure you haven't heard about him? The Gazette is always on about it.'

'Maybe, but between the two of us, only Eric picks up that local gossip tabloid.'

After their conversation, Anita went to find Eric in the garage. He'd already parked the car in and was now busy unloading their suitcases.

'You were right. It was dad.'

'Not sure whether it's wise to say, but… uhm… I told you so?'

'Yeah, savor the moment. You won't have many more. Anyway, he also mentioned our garden looked great, better than how we keep it usually. He was talking about this mystery flower man or so.'

'Oh yeah,' Eric looked up with a smile. 'The Night Gardener? He did ours too?'

'You mean, my dad was actually serious…' She couldn't really finish, what was the point, since Eric had walked outside already to check the garden.

'Sure, he did!' Like a kid he ran back to Anita. 'He did! He did!'

'He did what?' Anita was becoming slightly annoyed at the men in her life being so excited about such a weird thing.

'The garden, he did our garden. It looks great!'

Eric pulled Anita outside and dragged her along their driveway to the road. They then turned around to look at their garden to see a colorful display of daisies, azaleas, camellias, forget-me-nots in front of a big bougainvillea bush. It was utterly stunning.

'How couldn't we have noticed *that*,' Anita exclaimed stressing every single syllable of that sentence.

'Too busy staring at our open garage, I guess,' Eric mumbled.

After looking at the display for a few minutes, one of their neighbors came home from work. He pulled up right next to them.

'It's awesome, isn't it,' he said as he pulled down his window.

'Hey there, yes, it looks great. We only just noticed it.'

'Well, so did we not too long ago. Probably not till yesterday that we could see you'd been done too. You guys are the second house in our street already.'

'Only yesterday? Wow, how did he do that?'

'Well, he sure is a mystery man, if you're asking me.' Then the neighbor said good-bye and drove into his own place.

Anita and Eric went back inside to prepare some food. After all the excitement, neither of them felt like going out or having an elaborate dinner. They settled for some quick, oven-baked schnitzel with some peas and carrots, all from the freezer. A nice glass of red wine, a 1998 cabernet sauvignon from Australia's south-east accompanied their meal.

As they'd finished eating, both were still enjoying their wine. They laughed at their reactions earlier in the day and likened it to some silly moments in their favorite TV shows, or better, to some people they knew who'd react that way all the time.

'If only we could record our faces,' Anita said laughingly.

'Record? Hang on, we probably did!'

Eric ran off to find his security camera recorder. He pulled out a hard drive from the recorder on which all of that month's recordings were saved and connected it to his laptop. Taking another glass of wine, they made themselves comfortable on the couch and keeping the laptop on their laps. Eric found the recording of that afternoon, and both laughed at seeing their reaction play out like a comedy show.

'What about the mystery man? Would he be on there too?' Anita's face lit up with curiosity.

'Not sure, but we can try. It should've recorded everything in front of our house.' Eric said as he started looking through the files named by date and time. 'What did our neighbor say, they didn't notice until yesterday?'

Eric searched and searched. It wasn't the night before yesterday as nothing seemed to have happened. Their neighbors were probably just like them, too busy worrying about other things to notice the little bright things in life. Eric kept looking until half an hour later, he found a recording where they could see some movement and change in their garden.

As they both stared at the screen which played out that night's recording in black, white and grayscale, they were both amazed at the care the figure in the dark seemed to display for the plants in their garden. He'd trimmed the bougainvillea to shape cutting away dead branches. He then planted different flowers creating the sea of flowers they'd noticed earlier that day.

Finally, in the last five minutes of the recording where the man was busy sweeping up the cuttings on the driveway, they could see his face. It was a face of an older person. The man had a shortly trimmed beard and moustache. He had squinty eyes that seemed preoccupied. On his head he wore a large black hat; his full body was covered by dark clothing, boots and gloves.

They both gasped. They'd seen this face before. It was the retired man they'd often meet in the supermarket. They'd even spoken a couple of times about the weather and how plants would like it or not.

The next day, Eric took the recording straight to the Maleovale Gazette's editorial office. The editors and reporters were shocked and excited. They'd finally found the mystery gardener. Things went quickly from there: the newspaper was involved, the mayor was involved, and soon the whole town was involved.

Once identified, the man's name was Julian Ford, a large crowd led by the mayor and the Gazette's editor-in-chief gathered in front of his house. Everyone'd brought flowers from their gardens, well only those that had them, and as he opened the door the crowd cheered and showered him with flowers. It was the most beautiful sight, if ever you like flowers or confetti or the like raining from above.

The man was shy, but the mayor encouraged him to step forward and come outside of his house. As Julian stepped out, the mayor presented him with a spade, bought five minutes ago from the hardware store. The mayor's secretary had attached to the spade a bunch of flowers and key. The key wasn't gold plated, it was just a standard key. Because the secretary couldn't find a proper ceremonial key (most likely Maleovale had never ordered any), he used the spare key to the town hall's cleaning cupboard.

'With this, on behalf of the great town of Maleovale, the town in the valley of the Maleo River, where desert and grassland meet, I, the mayor of Maleovale, of the town in the valley of the Maleo River, where the grassland meets the desert, would like to give you this spade with the key to the city.'

The mayor obviously didn't have to give many speeches, but the crowd didn't seem to care. They all cheered as the mayor handed Julian the spade.

'Uhm… thank you, thank you,' he said timidly.

'So, dear Mr. Ford,' the mayor asked once the crowd had quietened, 'why did you do this?'

Julian looked at the mayor, then he turned his eyes to the crowd. He then looked at his feet.

'C'mon, you can tell us. Don't be shy.'

'Okay… uhm…, I did it because I like seeing that Maleovale looks like a nice place… uhm… like Leo von Eckdorf would have wanted it to look.'

He paused for a brief moment as everyone was listening intently. Tears started rolling over his cheeks. He then looked at the mayor.

'It was meant to be like a real paradise,' Julian continued, 'Von Eckdorf had it all planned out: a new Garden of Eden on the fringe of the desert. Only, his dream died with him as the mayor at that time and his council men decided that it would all be too expensive. I was a junior town planner at the time, but as my supervisor disagreed with the town's leaders, they made me in charge of town planning, maintenance and beautification. I followed the decision to change the town's design and looks, even though only a few years before, Leo von Eckdorf had all asked us in the town planning team to swear to him to follow his plans. I betrayed Leo and now I've betrayed all of Maleovale.'

'You haven't betrayed us,' the mayor said quickly, but he wasn't sure why as he didn't know what Julian meant. 'You've made our town look beautiful, look at the gardens you've brought back to life!'

'I only did those at night after I'd retired from my work at the town hall. I couldn't live with myself as being the one responsible for making the Garden of Eden fail into the nation's ugliest town. I wanted to bring Von Eckdorf's dream back to life.'

Everyone was stunned, and *no one* dared to say anything. Then the mayor, feeling as it was his duty, tried to comfort the old man.

'I'm sure Von Eckdorf would have loved how you've made his dream come true. I know everyone here agrees.'

The crowd broke out in a loud shout and cheered. From that moment on, Julian Ford was known as the Gardener of Maleovale, the one who made the vision of Leo von Eckdorf come true.

Afterward, the mayor decreed that more should be invested in making Maleovale a beautiful place again. The people also started taking better care of their properties. All around town the gardens blossomed and bloomed as people helped each other out; the ones that had greener fingers would help those that had none.

As for Julian Ford, he would still help in people's gardens. The mayor also appointed him to plan any projects that would undo the ugliness that was stingily introduced in the past. The first thing he did was to restore the Town Hall Plaza to its former glory – Leo von Eckdorf's statue would look again over its own Garden of Eden. And as for Eric and Anita Bloome, they'd enjoy theirs for many a year.

Beautiful gardens in the nation's ugliest town? How could that be? Which town could it be, anyway?

Not everyone likes gardening or has a garden that they can make into something that will truly stun everybody. It is definitely not the moral of this story to spur people on to do more gardening.

However, in a sense our lives can be like gardens. Sometimes we feel cluttered or overgrown as we feel like losing control over our own lives. Sometimes we feel like we achieve or produce little and it seems like there is too much dead wood and bushes can't produce flowers. Sometimes, even, we feel like our lives don't fit our personality and interests, like a garden that just doesn't fit the house; something feels like it's off, something is constantly bugging us.

It is good to be reminded that there are people around us that can help us. Oftentimes, these people are hidden in plain sight, or at least we don't notice what and how much they do for us. Our relatives or friends that support us or advise us when we just don't know what to do. These people are like mystery gardeners helping us tame the gardens of our life.

True encouragement is to stop and recognize these people and what they do for us. We often take their presence in our life for granted. But what if that person wouldn't have been there? How would we've lived? How could we get ourselves sorted?

It's important to also recognize them for all that they've done for us. This doesn't mean that we gather a crowd outside their house and organize the mayor to give a speech and a special token. It does mean, however, that from time to time we take time or make an effort to show our gratitude. Being grateful to these key people in our life is the best form of encouragement we can give them.

Gratefulness (*or* gratitude) is probably the best attitude we can take on in life. Coming from the Latin word *gratia*, gratefulness and the related *graciousness* and *grace* all imply something about kindness, generosity, receiving something for nothing, giving and receiving and the beauty of this[1]. It takes our focus away from what is bothering us to what is truly important in life. Our focus also shifts from all that we don't have to what we do have. It is an attitude of counting our blessings as opposed to worrying over our everyday needs or desires[2].

Anita and Eric were too focused on their opened garage, so that they didn't notice the paradise displayed by their garden. The town's council decided to focus on saving money, that they'd lost focus on the vision with which their town was developed. The result of their focus on the negative, their fear of losing any of their material belongings, led to Anita and Eric not even seeing the warm welcome left behind by Anita's dad. The town became the ugliest town due to its own disregard of beauty for the sake of saving money. Similarly, ungrateful people often show the least beautiful of attitudes.

Only when we stop ourselves from focusing on our own needs, and we start enjoying what we already have, we can become truly grateful people. We can enjoy the people around us and the beauty displayed by others. As a result, by being grateful and encouraging those that helped us, we are encouraged ourselves[3].

There is this story about a woman in the ancient near eastern town of Joppa who was always doing good. Her name was Tabitha[4]. She especially looked after those that others wouldn't care about: the poor and the widows. She made them new clothes, so that they could at least walk around in dignity. Just like in our culture, clothing told your stance in society, or to what group or class you belonged. By sowing new clothes, she literally upgraded these people that otherwise would have been regarded the lowest of society.

However, this woman fell sick, terribly sick. Her condition deteriorated so much that eventually she died. She was so loved for all she'd done that the people honored her with a washing and a wake before she'd be buried. In those areas, people are normally buried within a day due to the warm Mediterranean climate.

At that time in a neighboring town, one of the highly regarded leaders of Tabitha's group of people stayed as he was travelling through the area. His name was Simon, but people also knew him as Peter. Word was sent to him about this woman, what she'd done and how she'd passed away. He went immediately to Joppa to see her body.

As Peter arrived, widows from Joppa crying and sobbing surrounded him. They showed him all the garments and clothing made by this remarkable woman. She truly was an angel to them.

Then Peter did something remarkable of his own. He sent them all away and he knelt beside the body of this special woman. He prayed. Then he turned himself towards her body and said: 'Tabitha, get up.'

A miracle happened! She opened her eyes and Peter taking her by the hand helped her up. The others were called back in and they were stunned by what had happened. They all celebrated, especially the widows that had held her so dearly. They now got to show her their gratitude also while alive[5].

It is great to see how the people recognized the tremendous work done by this woman, that they honored her with a special viewing before the usual burial. It's great to see how people are fare welled with honor, even though their work in life wasn't always recognized. It would still be better if we could honor those people while they're still with us.

The people of Joppa received another chance to show their gratitude, their encouragement to this woman. They also received another chance to benefit from her goodness. Our chance to encourage those around us, that have helped us all this time, is now. Let's show them how much we appreciate them. You will see how this starts a new flow of encouragement and goodness being released both in their life and in that of your own. This flow will even reach others as they're inspired by how much support you've received (they wouldn't know about it either, unless they've been made aware about it by you) and the gratitude that you've shown[6].

For me the people that have supported me the most, are my parents. Without their help and investment in my life, I wouldn't be the person I am today. I know this all sounds cliché, but for me my attitude shifted significantly when I realized this.

It wasn't until I moved out from my parents' house to live on my own and study in Amsterdam. As I explained earlier, I was only seventeen years old. Before I moved out, I'd taken everything for granted in one way or another. I knew they didn't have much, and they'd made sacrifices to look after my siblings and me, but I never recognized the care and support they provided even in the littlest of things. Once I'd moved out I had to organize my own life, cook my own meals, do my own shopping and do my own laundry (however, I did regularly take dirty laundry home on the weekend, because no-one can give my clothes that clean smell as my mum could – that is the excuse I keep telling myself, to this day).

As soon as I realized all this, I recognized all the things they'd done for me in the past. It added an extra dimension to how I perceived their love for me. Until that time, I'd had regular fights and arguments with my parents, but after that it changed. Of course, there are disagreements as in any relationship, but now these only occur sparsely and seem trivial compared to their love, care and support.

To me, my parents, but also my siblings and other relatives, are the mystery gardeners in my life. My parents did the bulk of the landscaping and pruning. In a sense they still help me maintain my garden; they don't do the hard work anymore as that's now my personal responsibility, but they do advise me from time to time how to handle different situations or relationships.

Ever since I became more grateful for my family, I enjoy being around them more. It brought me closer to them and I can have more meaningful conversations. It wasn't that they weren't there for these conversations; the blame is entirely on me and my attitude. I simply wasn't ready. In addition, it also helped me change my perspective from living for myself and my own needs to that of living for others and building healthy, supportive relationships. In all this, my parents are now encouraged as they can see the return on their investment made in my life. Despite the fact I now live with my own little family at the other side of the world, we still like to find time to see and meet each other.

Let's be encouragers like flowers that spread beauty and a wonderful scent. There is no better scent we can spread than an attitude of gratefulness. Let's change our focus from our own wants and take time to recognize the people that helped grow these flowers in our life. Let's show them our gratitude. Who knows, how many more flowers of encouragement will start growing in the gardens of others around us. Together we can create a see of color in our lives, spreading the scent of gratefulness.

Flowers growing, flowers blooming,
Displaying color, spreading scents with rife.
Seas of color, griefs consuming.
Attracting bees, birds – others spreading life.

Gratitude, grace, and gratefulness,
How can we respond, how can we react?
Some undeserved bestowed on us.
Be encouragers, who gratuitously act.

"Every good and perfect gift is from above, coming down from the Father of the heavenly lights, who does not change like shifting shadows."
James 1:17, NIV.

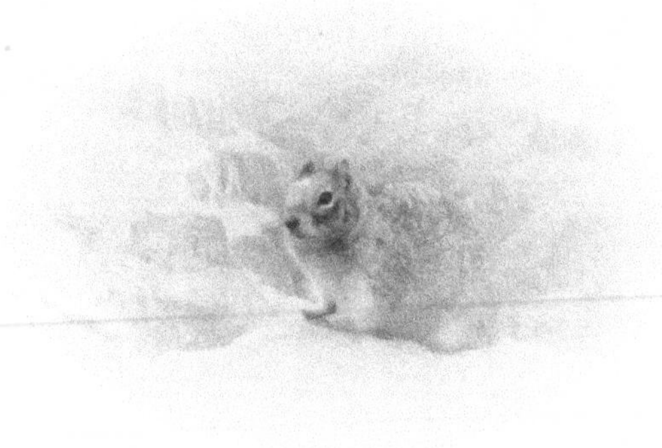

Rust, Screws & Muscle

"You give but little when you give of your possessions. It is when you give of yourself that you truly give."
Kahlil Gibran, *The Prophet*

Unexpected. Encouragement is like a car mechanic's workshop. Old and new car parts are stored in one corner, a large workbench with a rack for tools like wrenches, ratchets and nut splitters kept in another. In the middle of the workshop there is a two-post car hoist to lift cars and small trucks; next to it there is a pneumatic lift for motorbikes. This is a well-organized workshop.

Behind a rack with storage cans for engine oil, a glass window is visible. The window is actually part of a make-shift wall of cement sheets and glass panels. It separates the 'office' from the 'working' area. In this office a small desk fills the majority of the space; it is placed right in the middle. Two chairs, one on each side, a bin, a filing cabinet and a water station fill the remaining space.

A little desk lamp, an old clunky laptop, a catalogue of car parts and a dirty coffee mug are all placed on the desk's little available surface area. It obviously is not used as a desk for academic research or journalistic work. This is a desk primarily used for invoicing and placing orders; the really hard work is done outside of this space.

Jeanne runs this small workshop with passion and zeal. She treats it like her home. Her actual home is a small one-bedroom cabin right next to the workshop. However, she spends more time at work than anywhere else. Her cabin she only uses for cooking, washing and sleeping; most of her meals she has on the job anyway.

Jeanne doesn't work by herself. Kyle is a casual worker, who basically works fulltime at Jeanne's workshop. She never offered him a permanent contract; he never asked for it. One day, Kyle hopes to run his own place somewhere along a busy route in the country's west, as he loves the lifestyle there and hopes to run a big business. Till then, he works for Jeanne. Both are diligent and hard workers who deliver good work for a reasonable price.

Jeanne's workshop is located in a small town along a not-too-busy highway in the middle of the country. The highway leads north of the main east-west connecting freeway, opening the local agricultural area to the rest of the world. In this town, mainly working-class families live who depend strongly on the agricultural activities in the hinterland. Jeanne's business, likewise, services small farm trucks, pick-up trucks and other vehicles. Tractors she services on-site on any given farm.

Outside of the workshop, children often play with anything they can find. Screws, stones, twigs, random pieces of metal or the like. As they fossick around for anything they can use in their play, the kids regularly peak in the workshop to see if Jeanne's around. Kyle's not really great at chatting with the neighborhood children, but Jeanne always takes time to show them around the place, the cars she's working on, and hand them something they can play with.

One Saturday morning, some of the kids are already out playing, despite the cold wind picking up and blowing through the quiet town. Jeanne's workshop doors are ajar, probably she closed them to keep the wind out as normally she'd have them wide open.

The children walk up to the workshop and peak through the gap between the big, heavy timber doors. They can't see much as their eyes haven't adjusted to the dim light inside yet.

'Hey Jeanne!' one of the children calls out, 'are you there?'

No response, but there is the sound of a rattling chain.

'Hey Jeanne, is that you?' another one yells out. Normally she's pretty quick to respond.

Rattle, rattle… cloink!

The kids hold their breath. They're ready to jump away from the workshop doors, but then…

'Say what? Who there?'

It was Jeanne!

'Hey Jeanne, it's us, you know, us.'

'Who?' Jeanne squinted to see the silhouettes of people standing in the door. Little people with high-pitched voices. 'Oh, you guys! Come on in. Got to show you something.'

The kids walk into the dimly lit workshop. As their eyes adjust to the light, they see Jeanne leaning up against a small, rusty car. To the kids, the old-fashioned bonnet is shaped like a big tongue hanging between two poking round eyes: the car's headlights. Where the paint hasn't pealed, the car is a dusty yellow, the kind you find in sandy deserts, bleached by too much sun.

'Cool,' one child whispers.

'What's that piece of gunk?' another one says out loud.

The kids come closer and look all around the car from its googly headlights to its small rounded trunk at the back. They look at the classic wheels, the little old-fashioned wipers and the classy rounded sidemirrors.

'This piece of *gunk*,' Jeanne stresses the last word with disgust, 'is nothing other than an original 1971 Volkswagen Type 1 1302. A.K.A. the VW Beetle, but you can call her "Bug".'

'Cool,' one whispers again.

'I heard about them,' another one says, 'my grandad used to drive one. My dad told me that he secretly took them to Beetle races.'

'Beetle races? How could these pieces of gunk ever race?'

'Now you should stop saying "gunk".' Jeanne is slowly becoming annoyed with that "gunky" kid. 'You can race in any vehicle! But you can race even better with the right engine.'

'The right engine...?' the kids utter in combined confusion.

Jeanne couldn't help herself but to smile. 'Yes, the right engine makes a massive difference. Of course, the driver is important, too. But with enough power, your little car can win any race!'

'Are you working on the engine, then?'

'Sure I am. I've got this old rusty Ford Pinto in the back. I'll fix its engine and put that one in this beauty of a little Beetle... I'm just waiting for Kyle to come in.' Jeanne looks over the kids' heads to check if anyone was coming through the doors... She sighs, 'but he's late.'

'Can *we* help?'

'Err, I'm not sure...'

'I've helped my dad with building our shed,' one child jumps up before Jeanne can finish her sentence.

'I've helped my mum with fixing our washing machine,' another one excitedly exclaims.

'I'm not sure, I'm any good,' a third kid mutters, 'I haven't done anything like that. But,' a smile appears on his face as he continues, 'I'd love to learn.'

Jeanne is stunned by both the eagerness and the experience within the group. She quickly looks around and checks whether the workshop is in a safe working order for the kids to help her with anything. 'Well, uhm, okay, I guess.'

Together with Jeanne, the kids work hard and loud. Of course, they're playing around more than actually working, but nonetheless Jeanne takes her time to explain to the kids how the old Pinto's engine works and how it should look like. She also explains the different bolts used and how to tighten or untighten them using a wrench, how the pistons work, and much, much more. They actually managed to fix it before the middle of the afternoon!

'Okay, well done, kids.' Jeanne wipes off the sweat of her forehead as she leans back. 'We did it.'

'Cool,' one of the children says.

'Can we now pop it into the Beetle?' another one asks.

'Yes, I guess…,' Jeanne frowns as she's thinking how to proceed with the next step, 'but I can't ask you to help me with that. No, you definitely can't help with that.'

'Why not?' they ask as their disappointment is obvious.

'Well, it's not safe.' Jeanne thinks hard to not disappoint the kids even more. 'It's really heavy stuff. You first need to lift the old engine out and then lift the new engine in… Engines are heavy, they were made to deal with heavy forces. They shouldn't fall apart or jump right out of your car. You kids are too light, I need Kyle to help me with *that*.'

The children are still disappointed, but they get the point, at least for now. They start thinking about how long it would take before Kyle would help Jeanne, and before they can race in the Beetle with its new powerful engine…

However, before anyone could comment, Kyle finally walks in.

'*Heya* everyone!'

'Kyle?' both the kids and Jeanne say in one breath.

'Eh, yeah. I'm sorry I'm late… I had a big night and… I forgot to set my alarm.'

'Big night, eh?' Jeanne has a big grin lifting her left cheek. 'What've you been up to?'

'Eh, well, a mate had this party, and, yeah… I didn't get home till 6 in the morning.'

'6 o'clock!' Jeanne's eyes grow nearly twice their normal size. 'You know, I start at 6 in the morning?'

'Yeah… I know. I should've called, or I could've dropped by. I'm sorry.'

'I should've, I could've… well, that's all good and stuff, but nothing to help me here. I'm happy you're here now,' Jeanne says as she shrugs her shoulders. Another little smile escapes. 'I hope you're well rested, I really could use your strength now.'

Kyle helps Jeanne with the heavy lifting. They take out the Beetle's old engine and replace it with the fixed-up Pinto's one. It takes a lot of force, a lot of tinkering and a lot more time than expected. Before any of the work is completed, the kids must leave.

'Come back tomorrow after lunch,' Jeanne tells them as they leave, 'we'll take this little one out for her first ride!'

Kyle and Jeanne continue working till late in the night. Finally, right before the first sunrays touch the top of the workplace's roof, they finish tightening the last few bolts. Exhausted but satisfied, both Jeanne and Kyle go home and crash on their beds. Before long the kids will knock on their door, they can be sure about that.

That Sunday afternoon, the kids run out to the workshop. They can't hide their excitement. Some of their parents are curious and have come out to check out this Beetle with Pinto power for themselves.

Obviously, Kyle and Jeanne haven't had enough rest, but are too excited themselves to cancel the test drive. They, too, can't wait to experience the result of their hard work.

Everyone cheers with the first sound of the engine starting and revving. They take the 1971 Beetle out for her first ride, revigorated with the strength provided by its new beating heart. A true beauty she is, full of power and vigor. Of course, everyone must sit in it as Jeanne and Kyle take turns in driving the old car around. It sure is a team effort and a team enjoyment for everyone!

Encouragement is like a car mechanic's workshop.

As I'm thinking about this story, I can't help it but think about the famous little white Volkswagen Beetle with its own persona: Herbie. This sentient car with its yellow-on-black Californian license plate was the star in a number of movies and even had its own TV series. It was the champion in many a race and even the rescuer of a widow's home. This car has shown himself a true friend with its own heart of gold.

In this story we meet another Volkswagen Beetle. It's an unnamed car with a bit of rust and dust. We don't know much about it or what it has meant to its owners throughout the years. We don't know about its successes or its failures, when it broke down along the road or when it ran a flat tire. We don't know whether it was a hero too, or a failure, or just a good old car for every-day use, but somehow it is good enough to receive a second life with a new pumping heart: a Ford Pinto's engine.

A Pinto's engine is much stronger than that of a Beetle, but nonetheless it fits well as a replacement to this little Beetle. Its own heart and strength may have grown weary and can't keep up with the present race in life, but with a new heart, a new empowerment, it may actually be able to face another race.

The engine transplant is a success and the renewed car drives around town in a joyful test. It's got the potential now to win many a race, or to just be a more powerful car on the road. However, would it ever live up to this potential? Would it ever win? Would it be sold to another owner who just stalls it in a large collection of classic cars? We simply don't know, or ever will.

Nonetheless, it has been empowered. It has been revamped. It has been strengthened to face whatever the future holds for it.

The car isn't the only one in this story that is empowered and equipped for future success or challenges. We meet Jeanne, her assistant Kyle and the little, dusty town's children. Jeanne's teaching Kyle the ins and outs of her trade. She also gives him the opportunity to develop and grow in his own skills. Even though Kyle may have different ideas of future application of these skills, she's still mentoring him.

Also, and Jeanne probably isn't aware of this, she mentors the town's children. She takes the time to show what she is up to and how she is doing it. By role-modelling her skills to the kids, they must have learned a lot about cars, tools and skills.

And then there is Jeanne herself. Her skills did not develop overnight, nor did her patience and care. She must have learned it and someone else must have trained her. She, in turn, must have had a mentor, a role model, in this trade.

Looking at the skills, it is interesting that Jeanne's not only modelling the mechanical ones. She doesn't just show how a car works, or how to fix an engine. She doesn't just explain what the different tools are and how you can use them.

Jeanne also shows how to work hard, and how to keep working despite the size of the task or whether she is helped with it or not. She shows how to engage with someone who's just let you down, or how to move on after that. She models endurance, perseverance and grace.

How do we influence the people around us? Some we specifically train for a task as they're our apprentice, our student, or our assistant. Some we may not be aware of but are looking at us from close by or a far: our children, our siblings, our friends, our employees, our neighbors, our colleagues. We may not think that we're training *them* or educating *them*. However, the way we live our lives, the way we treat others, or the way we face the challenge at hand, it speaks volumes to those observing from the sideline.

In everything we do, act, behave or speak, we show others how they can do, act, behave and speak. We show them what we think is acceptable. We show them what we think is good. We also show them how they can show others.

Good and healthy role models show how to learn and apply skills the best way, but also how to engage with and value others and their contributions in an encouraging way. Good and healthy role models are encouragers; or let me turn this around: encouragers *are* good and healthy role models.

We all are on a journey. We all try to grow and develop, so that we can face the challenges that we face every day. We all want to cope; we all want to survive. Most of us want more, though, we want to thrive.

We all are finding our way. We all want to find out about our own strengths and our weaknesses. We all want to figure out how we can best harness them to live a life of accomplishment and fulfilment. We all want healthy relationships; we all want to be part of a strong, accepting and meaningful community.

The problem is, however, that thriving in life, or developing meaningful relationships isn't something that we know how to do from birth. Actually, unless we have good parents providing a healthy, stable home, we're at a disadvantage from the onset[1]. By nature, we are selfish, we are trying to survive. We can't thrive if our sole focus is to survive.

To develop healthy relationships, we need to learn to give of ourselves to others. To thrive in life, we need to come to a place of security where we know that we have enough to survive and no one is out there to get us.

We don't learn this from nature. We don't learn this by ourselves.

Someone must show us, someone must at least give us some direction. We *need* someone to show us or give us this direction. We need role models. We need mentors. We need someone who takes us under their wing and who we can follow on their journey. Their journey then in part becomes ours.

This reminds me of the story of the lone old wise man. His work was all about helping people see things from the right perspective, and pointing out major fallacies, especially in high-ranking leadership.

After a major breakthrough in his work (a breakthrough of the kind that would have allowed him to say: 'I told you so'), he'd encountered a serious setback. The setback was so severe, it was life-threatening. He fled to the wilderness, but also sank in a major circumstantial depressive episode.

The depression became too heavy – he couldn't see any meaning in anything he'd done. All he could see was to find a rapid end to it all. A rapid end to himself.

But then, in a rock crevice, a gap between ancient pillars of stone, he found meaning again. His work was not done yet. As long as he kept it to himself, his work's significance had long passed. However, when he would pass it on, it would find renewed meaning and the work itself would take off exponentially.

With renewed vigor, the lone old wise man travels to a little rural village. On one of the fields he finds a young man plowing the field. Two oxen yoked together pull a primitive device that is held down and steered by the man.

The old man walks up to him, takes off his mantle and drapes it over the young man's shoulders. It was a sign of 'follow me, join me on my quest and carry my work beyond where I can take it'.

The old man ended up instructing the younger one to share the workload with two others, one a military man, one a servant, both to become kings. The young man follows the older one's instructions, but that's not all. He ends up instructing and mentoring hundreds more. Truly taking the work beyond the old man's wildest dreams.

These two men became known in history as two of the greatest prophets in ancient Israel. They took on kingdoms and uprooted armies. How sad it would have been if the older one didn't pass on his calling to the younger one, all we'd have been left with was one change in the policies of a single kingdom and one really angry queen.

The greatness of Elijah only grew because he was obedient to encourage and empower the younger Elisha. To teach this young man all he had learned in his many years of service. To take him under his wing, or his mantle, so that Elisha could take it further[2].

When I look at my own life, I have had multiple role models. Some were better than others. Some teach you how to do things, and others how *not* to do it. Some people can only provide guidance in a short season in life, others stick with you for many years.

The most I've learned is from my parents and how they journeyed in life, their family and their community. I've learned from other relatives, teachers and youth workers[3]. In my academic life, my advisers and supervisors have contributed a tremendous amount of knowledge and wisdom, that you can't find in books. Without their advice, I couldn't have navigated the turbulent seas of academia.

However, when I'm most reminded about the importance of role models, is when I look at our little son. Although he's just a toddler, he loves showing that he is very capable of doing things himself. When he expresses this, I hear words and sayings, and sometimes even tones that only come from me. It's like I've got this little echo box next to me, returning the sound of my voice with a delay of days, sometimes weeks.

Our little man also likes to do the things I do. When I lay pavers to fix up our pavement in the backyard, he wants to dig the sand, carry a paver and tap it with a hammer (all in the fashion that befits a toddler, of course). When I paint the walls, he wants to hold the brush. When I sweep, clean or put things away, he has to do it, too.

In everything I do, say or go about my way, I know that I'm teaching my son. Whether the outcome is positive, is my choice and the fruit to be tested in due time. He's the one that will carry on what I've sowed into him and has the potential to multiply it beyond my wildest imagination. So, my hope is that it'd better be good.

Let's view others in our life this way. Let's be aware of the wisdom, knowledge and insights we learned over the years, the skills and techniques others have passed onto us, and the value and potential it all has when we share it with others an empower them to take it further. Let's be role models.

Let's be encouragers regardless the shape of our workshop. Let our lives, our journeys, our workshops welcome in others. Embrace them and intertwine our knowledge, wisdom and experience with theirs. Let's live out how to encourage others, how to build others up and show others the way in life. Let's be encouragers despite the rust, dust and scratches we gain in life. These are just the marks of a life lived in its fulness. Let's not withhold it from others. Let's be encouragers.

Screws and rust and a muddy road,
Relics and priests and truths of old.
None's to find life's truths on their own,
None's to kindle ambers unknown.

Making, fixing and going forth.
Praying, guiding, star of the north,
Ones enlightened us 'yond our way.
Ones showed how to us 'yond this day.

"The Lord himself goes before you and will be with you; he will never leave you nor forsake you. Do not be afraid; do not be discouraged."
Deuteronomy 31:8, NIV.

Whispers in the Wind

When you get into a tight place, and everything goes against you till it seems as if you couldn't hold on a minute longer, never give up then, for that's just the place and time that the tide'll turn. Never trust to prayer without using every means in your power, and never use the means without trusting in prayer. Get your evidences of grace by pressing forward to the mark, and not by groping with a lantern after the boundary-lines, — and so, boys, go, and God bless you!'

Harriet Beecher Stowe, *Old Town Folks*

Unexpected. Encouragement is like whispers in the wind, carried from distant places to regions far and wide. You don't know where they come from, or to where they are carried off. You don't know who uttered them and for whom they were meant to be. All you know is that you caught them in your ear. You intercepted the transmission. You received the message.

Whispers through a whirlwind of thoughts. Whispers through a storm that may rage on in your mind of things that vie for your attention. The business of life, the goals and the achievements. The desired prestige, the competition and the opposition. The worries, the anxieties and the despair.

Whispers traverse through this storm, through this whirlwind, and catch you off guard. They hit you as you didn't expect them they would. They challenge your focus. They draw your eyes from your surrounds to the finish line.

'There,' they say, 'there is your goal.' And: 'Come on. Come on, you can do this.'

It is when we start engaging with these whispers, we will find new strength. When we start a conversation, not a fight, with these whispers, that they draw something out of us, we didn't know even existed. Or, they impart something in us.

One of these conversations is like this:

'Come on. Come on you can do it.'

'I'm not sure. I'm tired. I've run so far.'

'Just another block. There, you see there is the turn already.'

'Okay, just another block. I can do it. After that, I can rest.'

'Don't just rest, now you've reached the turn. There, you see the next block is only 250 meters away. You can do those few meters still, can't you?'

'Okay, okay. I'll give it a go. Let's go.'

After a large number of blocks, the marathon runner reaches the turn that leads to the last half a mile.

'Come on,' the whispers continue in his mind. 'You've already come this far, you can't give up now.'

With renewed strength, the marathon runner gives his all. He exploits reserves of his energy he'd never thought still existed in his weary body. The whispers, they kept him going. The whispers, they unlocked the potential of these hidden wells.

He crosses the finish line and succeeds.

These whispers, they are generally soft spoken. Of course, otherwise they wouldn't be whispers. You need to tune in and listen carefully, otherwise the storm in its rage will overpower their voice.

If you listen carefully, you can hear not just the syllables or words uttered, but you can even distinguish voices. If you listen intently, you can distinguish different ways of speaking, nuances in expression and tone. It is as if different voices, different persons, are at the source of these whispers. Each person speaking in their own unique way.

One voice sounds very familiar. It's probably the sound that we are used to the most, and maybe even like the most. This voice can either cheer us on, or sometimes deter us from even commencing.

This voice speaks with the tone we'd use ourselves. The tone of happiness when we are happy. The tone of despair when hope seems lost. It speaks with the tone of our own voice.

The next voice, or maybe even group of voices we also recognize. They sound like our father or our mother. They sound like our siblings, or our friends, or others who've spoken into our lives. They encourage us or tear us down, depending on how they've treated us in the past.

The last voice is quieter and not easily linked to anyone we know in particular. Glimpses of this voice we may have heard in other people. But never can we label this voice with the name of anyone we know. It has its own unique sound, its own unique tone. It encourages us in ways that we could not have known; it shares wisdom that we couldn't have come up with ourselves.

This voice is softer and lovelier. At the same time, it speaks louder because it contrasts all other whispers and stormy winds the most. We may find that our own voice, and those of the people around us, can contradict and argue with this small whisper.

This whisper is caring and always seeks out the best for us. It is encouraging and always draws out previously unknown potential. It is loving and pursues us to love others, too.

Conversations with this small voice go like this:

'My child, you are not alone.'

'But I feel like I'm trying to hang on to this last bit of energy all by myself.'

'I am with you.'

'But this work, there's still so much work to do. I've been on it for months. My boss wants me to finish it soon, but it looks like I'm nowhere close to finishing. My colleagues have left me to my own devices; they've written me off. I'm all alone now... and I'm so tired.'

'Don't worry. Do what you can do. You're not in it alone. I'm right here with you and I know you can complete it. It may not be the best work ever, but is that really necessary? People may demand perfection, but will anyone ever reach that? How about, you do the best you can given the situation? I am sure you can do that.'

'I'm not sure. I've never delivered something I'm not completely satisfied with. I mean, I want to do something well, or not do it at all.'

'Well, then don't do it.'

'But that's the point. That is not an option.'

'Then do it well.'

'I'm trying to, but I can't do it anymore. I don't have it in me. It all seems lost.'

'Then do it the best you can. It is still better than everything else your colleagues have done, they've abandoned ship, they haven't made anything out of this.'

'But it will affect my performance...'

'In whose eyes? Your boss'? Probably he can't do anything better himself. Your colleagues'? You said yourself they'd left you with it. Or do you mean in your own eyes? Maybe you should try looking through mine.'

'What do you mean? I mean, what do you see?'

'I see my child who is tackling a big challenge. I see that the challenge you're dealing with is bigger than the task you're trying to fulfill. Your challenge is to let go of perfection and to be content with the best you can give. When you've given your best, enjoy it as your best. Don't try to be superman or wonder woman – someone you are not. You are my child; can't you be content with that?'

Another conversation goes like this:

'My child, you are not alone.'

'What?'

'You are not alone. My child, I am with you.'

'You are with me? You are with me? All I've seen so far is that you are *not* with me. You have left me like everyone else, and worse, you've taken everything from me!'

'Everything? Everyone?'

'Yes, everything and everyone.'

'What about the person at the checkout in the supermarket? Wasn't he nice to you?'

'What do you mean? It's his job. It's called customer service.'

'But he stayed nice, even when you didn't have enough money.'

'I said, it's his job. I'd complain if he wouldn't be nice.'

'Then, what about the person in the supermarket that chipped in five dollars for your groceries?'

'What do you mean? I didn't know the woman. She was just being kind.'

'She didn't have to? Or would you complain about her, too?'

'It doesn't matter. It was just a one-off, I'll never see her again.'

'What about the bus driver?'

'Again, it's his job to be nice...'

'And to let you on without paying for it? You didn't have enough money, remember?'

'Again, it's a one-off incident. Next time he'll make me pay – if I see him again, that is…'

'What about your landlord? He gave you another extension, he didn't have to, and you will see him again.'

Sigh. 'I can't argue with you, can I?'

'Well, you can always try. I won't get offended. As I said, I'm always here for you. I will never leave you. It may feel like as if the whole world is against you, or that everyone has abandoned you. No matter the feeling, I'm always sticking with you. It doesn't matter whether it's all your own fault, or whether you're a total victim. I'm with you no matter what. It is you that needs to become aware of that. It is you that needs to acknowledge my presence. Only then, you can face your challenges, and only then, you can get right up your feet. In the meantime, I'll be right here with you, waiting for you, to comfort you, to heal you and to restore you; to give you new strength.'

A whole other conversation goes like this:

'My child, I am with you.'

'Not now. Can't you leave me alone. I'm in pain.'

'I know, that's why I am letting you know that I'm with you. You aren't alone.'

'But you didn't do anything about it. You just let it happen. You just let them hurt me, betray me, backstab me. It hurts, you know. It hurts so much…'

'…'

'You see. Now you know how much it hurts, you are silent.'

'…'

'I *thought* so. Just leave me alone in my misery.'

'I'm still here, though.'

'You still here? Why didn't you say something?'

'I'll never leave you, no matter what you say to me or think about me. I'm always here, ready for you to embrace you in my arms.'

'Why didn't you embrace me when they hurt me? Why didn't you protect me, or at least warn me about their plans to use me for their own selfish goals?'

'I was there with you just as I am here with you right now. I was there to embrace you and to tell you, but you didn't want to take time to come to me and listen.'

'You could at least have stopped them or intervened somehow.'

'I could, but would that really be loving? You aren't a puppet, are you? And

I'm not a puppeteer, pulling your cords at every stride and keeping you to the script. You are my child, and just like any good parent, I let you make your own decisions whether the consequences are good or bad.'

'You could at least take away the hurt.'

'I can, that is why I am here with you.'

'And you can at least let them hurt. Isn't that justice?'

'Justice is a whole lot bigger than payback. Yes, everyone will be judged, but they will be judged fairly. Judgement and revenge are not the same.'

'Still I hope that they will rot in their own troubles.'

'Did you want to stop hurting?'

'Yes, I do. I'll feel much better when they suffer for all they've done.'

'Will you really? As I see it, everyone will be hurting in the end. You suffer because of the hurt they caused you. When they suffer, this won't ease your hurt, it will only make it look less bad.'

'Well, less bad is good enough for me. As long as they've had payback.'

'Less bad good enough? Really? I thought you wanted to stop hurting. I thought you wanted to be healed. Don't you understand, that as long as you hold onto your own grudge, you're holding onto your own pain?'

'What do you mean?'

'As long as you're holding onto your grudge, your desire for revenge, your judgement against the others, you are reliving the pain of the bad over and over again. It is like an open wound that, as soon as the blood dries and a crust forms, you dig it open with the nails on your dirty hands. The wound becomes infected and you're worse off than before.'

'How can I heal, then?'

'Release it to me. Just give it all to me.'

'Give what? How?'

'Give your pain to me and all your hurts. Surrender your grudge to me and your desire for revenge. Everything that you have against them, give it to me. Just leave it all with me and up to me.'

'But that is weak. I mean, I just give up. I just let them walk all over me.'

'No, that is not what it is. It is you allowing me to be your doctor, to surrender your own ways of trying to fix things and letting me clean it all out and dress it in my love. You will always retain the memory, which will make you wiser and stronger, but you won't have the pain or weakness. You can see clearly, not whilst torn by pain. You can better judge the situation and help yourself and others avoid it. If you're still stuck in your pain, your judgement is clouded, and you will be more likely to fall in the same trap again.'

'So, you mean, I should forgive? Forgiveness is weakness.'

'Yes, forgiveness is releasing all your pain, hurt, judgement and desire for revenge. It is letting them off the hook for what they did to you personally, but it is not letting them off the hook from justice. It is not weakness. Weakness is keeping the situation the way it is and let it grow in bitterness and despair. Strength is when you overcome your own pain, your own self-righteousness, and surrender it to me. Strength is to trust me that I will heal you and restore you, but not at your terms.'

'But then everyone could just do whatever they want. Where is justice?'

'Justice will happen, when you turn it around. If everyone would forgive, people won't act out of old hurt and react to others out of bitterness. People will look at each other with clearer eyes, with eyes of love and respect. Do you want to hurt someone you love and respect?'

'But people hurt each other even if they love them?'

'Hurt by someone you love is the most painful, I know. However, where forgiveness is, love can be restored, and it can grow even deeper. It hurts to till the soil; it's hard work, but without it, the crops can never grow their roots deeper and grow stronger. The harvest would look grim without the hard work preceding it. Hurt in a loving relationship can turn into hard labor that precedes great fruitfulness, only if the plant of relationship can be restored through forgiveness.'

'Hurt by someone you love is the most painful, I know. However, where forgiveness is, love can be restored, and it can grow even deeper. It hurts to till the soil; it's hard work, but without it, the crops can never grow their roots deeper and grow stronger.'

﹩℃

Sometimes, the greatest motivation and encouragement don't come from the outside, from others, but from the inside. Our thoughts shape us. René Descartes famously stated: *'Je pense, donc je suis'* ('I think, therefore I am')[1]. We are thinking beings. Everything we observe and undertake is attached to a thought. All our choices are considered in our thoughts.

Our mind is a powerful asset. Without it we can't achieve what we have, or we can't do what we want. If we can think it, we can (at least attempt to) reach it. In it lies an untapped mountain of creativity and will power.

We can be our own greatest encouragers. We can spur ourselves on to go beyond our best achievements, or above others' highest expectations. The key to transform the way we go about in life and to persevere through trials and challenges, lies within ourselves.

However, we can also be our greatest critics. We know our own motivations; we know why we do things. We also know how we should have done things and where we failed.

I am guilty of immense self-critique myself. If you ask my wife, my parents, my siblings, you name it, they will tell you that I am quite a perfectionist. If you don't believe them, check my personality test results. The first thing that pops up is "perfectionism". It's a great asset to do highly sensitive finetuning of the most delicate of scientific testing, but it's not great in real life.

Because of this perfectionistic trait, I often lack the joy that comes with achievement. I often think about how I could have done things better. I am constantly assessing how I could improve or make things more efficient. Again, this is good to excel in scientific precision, but it debilitates me in the rest of my life.

By constantly living a life of self-critique, I have become very self-aware and full of self-doubt. Thoughts go through my mind that constantly shift to what could have been, or what could be, that I can't see the beauty in what is and what has been. It is a life filled with worry.

The technical term is *rumination*, the fearful thoughts that dwell on the unknown, failures of the past or the perceived challenges in the future[2]. They don't just dwell on these things, but they keep dwelling; they keep constantly cycling through these worrisome aspects[3].

The biggest issue with rumination is, that it is completely useless. It doesn't help us overcome the challenges, or it doesn't help us deal with our failures. It only creates victims in the process: our joy, our happiness, our look on life, our hopes, our dreams. Once these have been shattered, we're left with fear, anxiety, despair and eventually depression.

Unfortunately, we aren't the only ones that are affected by all this. Our relationships will be strained; the ones closest to us we tend to push away. Others struggle to understand what is going on with us. We ourselves can barely understand ourselves. Eventually, families and friendships can break down.

Our minds, in their most critical of states, can be our own destroyers. They can be the strongest in pulling us down, in a way no outside force can.

That is maybe the greatest conundrums in life: our minds and their power to do good and to do evil. There is this tension: to keep spurring ourselves on to be the best person we can be and to excel in what we do, but not to give in to perfectionism and judgement of punishing ourselves for all we did or could do wrong. This is a constant battle in all of us, perfectionist or not, but definitely a real one for the more perfectionism-inclined.

That is why we need help. We need another voice in our lives that fully understands what we are capable of but does not judge us harshly. *Self-compassion* can help with this in a long way[4]. In a sense, self-compassion is looking at yourself through the eyes of a compassionate outsider. It is as if you're looking at yourself through someone else's eyes who thinks the best of you, who wants to help you get through and succeed.

I can try to look at myself and my situation more positively if I start seeing myself through someone's eyes, who really means well with me. Sometimes, I do this when I'm starting to feel anxious. I sit back and reflect how someone else would look at me, who wants the best for me but who is not involved in the situation at all. I find that, in that moment, my surging heart rate drops, and I can start to breathe again.

However, this only works for me in a limited way. Sometimes my perfectionism is too strong, or my worry too great. They tend to pull me back in the dark whirlpool of negativity and fear.

Or, sometimes the negativity piles up. At those times, I receive denials on job interviews, refusal of much-needed funding for further research and rejections of manuscripts for publication – all painstakingly prepared and put together. The things that carried my hopes for a brighter future, shattered to pieces. It seems like everything has been taken from me and I lost all ability to move forward.

Then, I need someone truly external to me to start speaking in my life. Then, I need true outside-help from someone who truly knows me, not just a pretended external view.

I have found that this truly objective, but compassionate and loving voice comes from my Creator. I have found that the most loving and well-meaning words spoken in my life come from the Father of life.

You may disagree with me on his existence, and just think of this as a little bridge to effective self-compassion. I won't hold it against you and I don't want to fight you on this. After all, I'm just sharing my personal experience.

How do I know that these "external views and words" come from my Heavenly Father? Usually, these words drop in my minds, these thoughts trickle in, when I least expect them. They are always overwhelmingly loving, more loving than I could ever be to myself or anyone else, not even to my wife and son. And, these thoughts are filled with ideas and words that I couldn't have come up myself.

These words gently pop in my mind and encourage me to not give up hope. They remind me that everything has a purpose. The jobs won't suit me and eventually would frustrate me. The funding will come from a different source. The manuscripts just need a better pitch to become more effective as research articles.

They are words of hope when all hope seems lost. They are words from a higher hope, a hope you don't think anyone would have naturally. In a sense, they speak of something above the natural, something *super*natural.

It isn't always easy to finetune myself to the voice of my Heavenly Father. I admit, often I don't even want to listen to this voice. Sometimes, I just want someone to agree with my anger and bitterness. Of course, staying bitter won't resolve anything and I feel worse.

Nonetheless, this voice keeps speaking and when I do tune in, I find relieve. I find the bitterness slowly losing its sting. I find comfort. Healing can start.

Listening to this voice doesn't come naturally, though. We aren't born with a special ability for heavenly wavelengths. As a matter of fact, the circumstances we find ourselves in and all the voices of the people around us are too strong.

We need to start engaging with our Creator before we can recognize his voice. We need to get to know him, we need to get acquainted. Jesus, my greatest inspiration, often talked about the Heavenly Father. He also said, that he is the good shepherd taking care of his sheep. As any flock with its shepherd, his sheep would be able to recognize his voice, simply because they're so familiar with him.

To become a true encourager, I'd like to encourage you to tune in with the greatest Encourager of all. I'd like to encourage you to get to know this Encourager. Start talking to him and then start listening. See what voices you can distinguish: your own, the people around you, and then this really loving, hopeful voice.

Once you've quieted yourself down and tuned into this still voice, start listening. Let the words flow over you. Hand this voice your pain and sorrow, all your rejection. Then, open yourself to receive his love and acceptance.

As you become more familiar with this voice, with every situation stop to listen to this voice first. When you see someone, listen to what this voice says about encouraging this person. When you see someone you totally dislike, or who has hurt you, listen to this gentle voice first. Let the words wash away negativity and bitterness and start encouraging. Sometimes, this takes a bit of time, so the best is maybe to not say much. A simple "hi", "hello" or other form of acknowledgment may be enough.

I know it isn't easy. Believe me, I know. I'm still struggling with this. Nonetheless, I truly believe the key to better relationships and to becoming genuine encouragers is to do exactly this.

We may know how to be the best encouragers – *in theory*. We may know that we should be present in the moment, listen to people and be a support, or be grateful and show this to those around us. We may even understand the need to have the best role models, but if on the inside we hold on to our pain and grudges, we simply can't be the best encouragers we could ever be.

Our intentions may be good, we may even do a good job encouraging others around us. However, if someone touches that sore spot in our lives, things change.

Whether it's the person that hurt us in the first place, or someone completely different, but they or their actions just remind us of the pain, the bitterness pops right up. Unfortunately, in those instances as the bitter pain shoots out with a big sting, we often can't control ourselves, and we will be remembered as *anything but* encouraging.

There is this ancient story about a person chosen to warn a big city of impending disaster. As this city was the capital of an enemy empire, this chosen man refused to go. He'd be too glad if that city would be destroyed and all his enemies along with it. After all, this empire was known as the most gruesome in all of history, and actually still is.

The man of warning left his town but travelled in the opposite direction. Instead of taking the road to the city, he took the boat to a distant land. However, a storm overran the boat and as an appeasement sacrifice the sailors threw the man overboard where the roaring waves swallowed him.

As the man was tossed around in turmoil in the raging sea, a sea creature swallowed him hair and all. There, in the belly of the beast, the man came to his senses. He now knew how it was to be in trouble. He knew how it feels when one's life is about to end by disaster. He finally surrendered and prayed.

By a miracle, the sea creature sick to his stomach of his unnatural meal, spat out the man. From then on, the man found his way to the city he was sent to in the beginning. He warned the city and all its inhabitants of the impending disaster.

After completing his task, he withdrew to a safe spot, but he kept the city within viewing distance. As it was a pretty hot place, he welcomed the immensely rapid growth of a bush that happened to just be planted, and providing shade, right next to him. A more comfortable and safer seat to view the impending spectacle he couldn't find, or wish.

Then the unavoidable disaster happened. It suddenly struck as rapidly as the miracle shading plant had grown. No one expected that such a tiny thing could have such immense repercussions.

It was a worm! A worm so tiny, but so hungry. It ate its way through the entire structure in such a rapid fashion, no man or beast could have ever stopped it. Within such a short time as the worm is small, the plant withered and died.

Angry, shouting and raising his fist to heaven, the messenger rages and vents all his frustration. He had to endure *all this* suffering! He had to go through *so much* turmoil. And for what? To find out that all his comfort was taken away and the city, his archenemy, was still standing. This is *completely* unfair!

This man, the prophet Jonah, was then reminded by this gentle voice about the love the Creator had for both Jonah and all his creatures in the Assyrian city of Nineveh. He loved Jonah to give him so many chances and even provided this beautifully shaded place. Nonetheless, he also loved the city, its people and its livestock, that when they turned away from their cruel unrighteousness, they received mercy and their lives were spared.

This remarkable story of Jonah is a well-loved tale, but its significance is often overlooked. More remarkable than him being swallowed by a fish (or a whale – let's not go into this discussion here) is that it was written pretty close to Jonah's lifetime, in the time of King Jeroboam II of Israel when sympathy for Assyria was extremely low after it had destroyed so many neighboring nations and even some of Jonah's kinsmen. It is remarkable then that they are presented as the unsung heroes, the people that actually do the right thing with the right heart.

Jonah's heart wasn't set on showing compassion, or on bringing out the best in others. He was reluctant to share the message of warning in the first place because he knew that the chance existed that they would be saved.

Throughout the story, we see that Jonah isn't concerned much with others, even though he sacrificed himself out of petty for the sailors. He knew that as a prophet he was called to help people find the right way in life, to help them reach their potential and stay safe. He knew the heart of the Creator, the loving Father of all the living. He knew that judgement wasn't there as a punishment to remind people of how bad they are, but as an unavoidable destructive consequence unleashed because of all the injustice caused by the judged. That's why he refused to bestow such grace on the city of Nineveh, the capital of the enemy of his people.

Let's not just only tune in to the voice of the source of all that exists, but let's also take heed of the words spoken. Let the message they carry touch us, and let the love and grace transmitted transform us.

Let this still voice speak into the core of our being. Let it touch and mold our perception of our identity. That is why I like especially the expression of Heavenly Father, or Father of all creation, as it emphasizes the role a father has in a child's life. A child's relational identity, the way they see themselves in relation to others and how they interact, is supported especially by a father who is lovingly involved in his child's life.

Let our relational identity be formed and transformed by the love and care of our Heavenly Father who longs to be involved in our lives. His words are words of love, grace and encouragement; they are never meant to tear us down.

We often read the stories about the Old Testament prophets as stories of an angry God seeking to punish and destroy all the little, ugly people doing such ugly things. The story of Jonah, one of the oldest prophetic stories, reminds us that these stories aren't anything like that.

The prophets themselves familiar with their Maker's voice, knew the heart behind their message even though it was often hard to bear. They knew that destruction and judgement were terrible, but they were the logical consequences caused and unleashed by evil actions. They also knew that the messages were sent to warn people of the impending disaster so that they could change their hearts and actions and find safety again.

Now, we know our own hearts, our own motivations and the reasons behind our own actions. We can only judge for ourselves whether they are based on love, grace and acceptance, always seeking the best in others, or whether they are based on pain, grief or rejection, always comparing ourselves to others and trying to find ways in which we can feel better about ourselves.

Let's be true encouragers and build others up, simply because we care about people and want to see them succeed. Let this still voice of love and grace slowly wash away our pain and bitterness, let it build and strengthen our relational identity. Let it encourage us, so that we can truly encourage others without any ulterior motives.

Let's be true people of encouragement!

Whispers traversing waves, whirlwinds and woe.
A still small voice
from a hardened heart heaving heavy load,
Restoring hope.

Love and grace break bitterness and worry.
A gentle voice
Touches, transforms and toils without tally
Encouraging.

"I have told you these things, so that in me you may have peace. In this world you will have trouble. But take heart! I have overcome the world.'
John 16:33, NIV.

Final Thoughts

U nexpected. Encouragement is such a powerful and valuable force that exists in the exchange between people. Unfortunately, it is often also the most neglected and undervalued.

Let's decide to change that perception within our lifetime. Let's leave a legacy to generations to come that is marked by encouragement firmly set in any conversation, interaction and partnership. What if we were known for being the generation that made the world a more encouraging place?

Instead of shattered dreams, we have people pursue their God-given call in life. Instead of living in a vertical, hierarchical society, people come alongside one another and view others as extensions and enrichments of their own shared journey.

Like a squirrel in the Grand Canyon surprises fatigued hikers by popping up unexpectedly, even though they're so common there, it is unexpected to *not* see them at all. Let's be people who surprise others with our encouragement, even though it is unexpected to *not* receive any encouragement at all.

I'm not talking about constantly going around and praising every person. I'm not pleading for a place where every dream is valid and worth pursuing. As a true encourager, you can see the difference. You can help steer people away from actually futile efforts. However, never in a way that puts the other down, but in such a way that they find a new dream, one worth the effort and to the benefit of many.

I'm not advocating for coddling people and creating an environment where the next generation lacks resilience. However, when truly encouraging people, you build rapport with the other. You'll have their trust that you're in it for their benefit, even though the talk may be tough, or the treatment stern. But don't think that you can just treat people harshly from the outset, and then expect that they trust your heart for their cause. Encouragement builds your relationship with the other; once this relationship is strong, you can challenge them more sternly as long as it remains clear it's for their own benefit.

Treat others as you yourself would want to be treated by them. That is the golden rule that never expires.

Let's be encouragers by taking time for others and giving them our full attention. Let's support them in their challenges and cheer them on in their efforts. Let's live lives filled with gratitude. Let's share our journey with others and share with them our gained wisdom and skills. Let's keep encouraging ourselves, not putting ourselves down, but also being refreshed by the encouragement of our Creator, the Father of all those who are alive.

Jesus of Nazareth, who in plain language and remarkable stories encouraged people, reflected the heart of our Heavenly Father. He clearly showed us what it's like to engage with people others didn't think it worth their time. He accepted the outcasts. He built up the lowly across the social divide with contempt for social norms. Let's follow his example and become people of encouragement. *Let's make encouragement the expected norm.*

"And you know that God anointed Jesus of Nazareth with the Holy Spirit and with power. Then Jesus went around doing good and healing all who were oppressed by the devil, for God was with him."
Acts 10:38, NLT.

Appendix 1 - How to be a Good Mentor

Being a mentor is more than being a person who encourages others, you are like a guide to them. I've had the pleasure of mentoring quite a number of people both pastorally and academically. In all instances, I found that if I just encouraged people once, they just felt overwhelmed. If I actively guided them, however, they would find their way themselves eventually. Remember, guiding is not telling people what to do, it is just pointing them in the right direction.

Being a mentor requires great listening skills. Without the ability to listen to people without jumping in to tell them how to fix or solve it, you can't be a mentor.

Search for a heart connection. You can't be a mentor if you don't understand the thoughts and motivations of the person you're trying to coach. You need to view, respect and understand them as the person that they are.

Care for the person you are trying to mentor. If you don't care about them as a person and about how they're doing in life, you may as well just employ them and be their boss, or fire them and not deal with them at all. You wouldn't care either way anyway. *A mentoring relationship is a caring relationship.*

Put yourself in their shoes. Try to understand their viewpoint, their frustrations or excitement. Think back to the time when you were sitting on their side of the conversation. How did the world look like to you back then? You need this viewpoint before you can guide them further beyond it.

Think of strategies how to guide them beyond the point they're at. Will you encourage them to think outside the box? Will you take them on a road trip to show them different places and vantage points? Or do you let them talk through their thought process and, with just a few questions, have them find their way beyond it themselves? These are all legitimate mentoring strategies. They all have in common, that you make them think differently without forcing them.

Be available. Don't think of all the other tasks you need to do after catching up with them. Don't worry about other business that still needs your attention. Don't just leave it with a single catch-up and one email, after which you lose touch. Be genuinely available, present in the moment when you meet them, and always ready to follow up.

Make time. Being available is more than just being present to them, it is also about taking the time to see them or speak to them. Being a mentor is probably the best thing you could do with your time, other than spending it with your family. You multiply yourself in other people, passing down wisdom, skills, experiences and your passion. A better investment of your time, I can't think of, so make time!

Practice these things and you will find out that the relationship will guide itself. You'll be a great mentor and the people you guide will benefit greatly.

Appendix II - Encouraging Acts

It doesn't need to cost much financially but being an encourager does demand your time and attention. Here are different ways, you could actively seek to encourage others.

- Put your phone, book or calendar down and take time for the other. Be totally available to them in that moment.

- Show the other that they matter, by starting your response by repeating in your own words what they've just told you before. This active listening trick helps not only build up the other, but also improves your own listening skills.

- Write a note about what you liked about what the other did or said. Leave it at their desk, on their car or next to their phone.

- Send a card with more than "greetings, such and such", but write a personal message. Put a stamp on it and mail it the old-fashioned way.

- Send a thoughtful text message.

- Take the other out for coffee or lunch and talk about nothing other than the other's interests.

- Ask the other, when they encounter a challenge, firstly what they think they need to do about it. Secondly, ask them how you can help supporting them.

- Call the other and ask how they're doing. What challenges them and what gives them joy?

- Point the other to actually helpful resources (those with proper sources, not hearsay posted by a friend of a friend) or guide them even toward professional help if you're concerned about their welfare.

- Only when you've at least taken time and your attention to apply six out of the above-mentioned acts, buy the other a gift. Always accompany your gift with a thoughtful and hand-written note (in your own handwriting!). *I know these can be harsh instructions for some employers or managers.*

Notes

Introduction

[1] Some stories from ancient story tellers are still being alluded to, whether for entertainment or for some deeper meaning. That is the reason Thomas Bulfinch (1796-1867) compiled these stories and published them in his three-fold work: *The Age of Fable, The Age of Chivalry* and *Legends of Charlemagne*, which I accessed in *Bulfinch's Complete Mythology (2000)* London: Chancellor Press. Great authors like J.R.R. Tolkien and C.S. Lewis continued this tradition and, not only allegorized entire worlds, but filled them further with stories to provide meaning to the people that inhibeted those worlds. In the Preface of The Age of Fable, Bulfinch appropriately cites the lines of Coleridge in *"The Piccolomini,"* Act II, Scene 4:

> *"The intelligible forms of ancient poets,*
> *The fair humanities of old religion,*
> *The Power, the Beauty, and the Majesty*
> *That had their haunts in dale or piny mountain,*
> *Or forest, by slow stream, or pebbly spring.*
> *Or chasms and watery depths; all these have vanished;*
> *They live no longer in the faith or reason;*
> *But still the heart doth need a language; still*
> *Doth the old instinct bring back the old names;*
> *Spirits or gods that used to share this earth*
> *With man as with their friend; and at this day*
> *'Tis Jupiter who brings whate'er is great,*
> *And Venus who brings everything that's fair."*

[2] See for example *Aristotle, Politics 1245b* and *Rhetorics 2:20.* In the latter, the Greek *paraboleh* (from which we gained the word "parable") is distinguished from the "fable", although is grouped with it.

[3] An interesting examination of the way early Rabbis applied parables is given by *Cave, C.H. (1965) "The Parables and the Scriptures" New Testament Studies 11: 374-387.*

[4] Although the early Church Fathers' allegorizing of Jesus' parables was often overdone and out-of-context (Augustine's allegorizing of the Parable of the Good Samaritan is a good example of this, see *Quaestiones evangeliorum 2.19*), a persistent, too critical attitude of rejection of anything symbolic was only started with the work of *Jülicher, A. (1888-1899) Die Gleichnisreden Jesu (two vols.), Tübingen: J.C.B. Mohr.*

[5] A good overview of parables and their interpretation, and which the following questions are based, is given by *Anderson, G.P. (2013) "Parables" in: Green, J.B., Brown, J.K. & Perrin, N. (eds.) Dictionary of Jesus and the Gospels, Downers Grove, Il: Inter-Varsity Press: 651-663.*

Food for Thought

[1] Read more about Zacchaeus in Luke 19:1-10 (Holy Bible).

Lifting Weight

[1] See Deuteronomy 25:17-18 (Holy Bible).

[2] Read more about Moses, Joshua and the Amalekites in Exodus 17:8-16 (Holy Bible). Maybe even the worst thing about it all was that the people of Amalek were related to the Israelites (see Genesis 36:12, Holy Bible). They were an Edomite tribe, descendants of the Edom's grandson Amalek. Edom, or Esau, was the brother of Israel (Jacob), so basically, Amalek was Israel's grandnephew. Talking about having a caring family?

[3] *Feeney, B.C. & Collins, N.L. (2015) "A New Look at Social Support: A Theoretical Perspective on Thriving Through Relationships" Personality and Social Psychology Review, 19(2): 113–147.* This article provides some great insight on the importance of relationships within families to provide a support network that helps people thrive in both adversity and in deciding on opportunities.

Hidden Treasure

[1] *Pruyser, P.W. (1976) The minister as diagnostician: Personal problems in pastoral perspective. Philadelphia: Westminster Press, p. 76.*

[2] See *Emmons, R.A. & McCullogh, M.E. (2003) "Counting Blessings Versus Burdens: An Experimental Investigation of Gratitude and Subjective Well-Being in Daily Life" Journal of Personality and Social Psychology, 81(2): 377-389* for an interesting study on how being grateful positively affected people's well-being and emotional outlook in life.

[3] *idem.*

[4] Tabitha was her Aramaic/Hebrew name, in Greek she was known as Dorcas.

[5] This story can be found in Acts 9:36-43 (Holy Bible).

[6] *Bartlett, M.Y. & DeSteno, D. (2006) "Gratitude and Prosocial Behavior – Helping When It Costs You" Psychological Science 17(4): 319-325.* This study shows that by being grateful for what someone has done for us, we tend to help others (i.e. strangers) more, too. It is not just the learned behavior that it is good to help others that makes us do it in the first place; having a sense of gratitude in itself is the first cause to encourage others and build stronger relationships-.

Rust, Screws & Muscle

[1] The first stage in becoming a leader actually happens in the family home, how conversations happen around the dinner table. The way family shares together and passes information about their day-to-day is formative for the way a child grows into leadership at a later stage in life. See *Banks, R. & Stevens, P. (eds.) The Complete Book of Every-Day Christianity: An A-Z Guide on Following Christ in Every Aspect of Life (1997). Grand Rapids, MI: Eerdmans: 231-235.*

A shorter excerpt of this is presented on pp. 194-195 of *Banks, R. (2009) "The Formation of Future Leading Servants" in: The Three Tasks of Leadership: Worldly Wisdom for Pastoral Leaders. E.O. Jacobsen (ed.), Grand Rapids, MI: Eerdmans: 191-201.*

[2] Read more about Elijah and Elisha in 1 Kings 18-19 and 2 Kings 2 (Holy Bible).

[3] My experience in learning about the importance of role modelling in leadership has been two-fold. Firstly, it was those who led me during my formative years, and the way they invested in me. Secondly, I learned a lot from a great resource that every leader and minister in children's, youth and even young adults' ministries should turn to from time to time: *Fields, D., Purpose Driven Youth Ministry (1998), Grand Rapids, MI: Zondervan.*

Whispers in the Wind

[1] *Descartes, R. (1637) Discours de la Méthode Pour bien conduire sa raison, et chercher la vérité dans les sciences. Leiden: Jan Maire.* Descartes later on wrote the same sentence in Latin: "Cogito, ergo sum."

[2] Suggestions have been made to separate rumination from worry with the former dealing with the past and the latter with the future; however, here I assume the two are closely intertwined and coupled as suggested by *Gu, J., Strauss, C., Bond, R. & Cavanagh, K. (2015) "How do mindfulness-based cognitive therapy and mindfulness-based stress reduction improve mental health and wellbeing? A systematic review and meta-analysis of mediation studies" Clinical Psychology Review 37: 1-12.*

[3] This dwelling or cycling through on the same negative thoughts is also termed "brooding"; see *Gu et al. (2015) idem.*

[4] Self-compassion has been shown that it can help depressed people to reconsider themselves a bit more positively; see *Diedrich, A., Hofmann, S.G., Cuijpers, P. & Berking,*

M. (2016) "Self-compassion enhances the efficacy of explicit cognitive reappraisal as an emotion regulation strategy in individuals with major depressive disorder" Behaviour Research and Therapy 82: 1-10.

Illustrations

All illustrations were of my own design. However, for the illustration belonging to *Food for Thought*, I used elements created by Renata.s (bridge) and Fanjianhua (silhouettes), available through Freepik.com. For *Rust, Screws & Muscle*, the illustration's base photograph is from Ryan McGuire, available through Pexels.com.

About the Author

Jozua van Otterloo is a scientist, Christian thinker and pastor. He is passionate about uncovering treasures in nature, but also helping people uncover treasures in their own lives. He loves to see the next generation fulfill its true potential.

He was born in the Netherlands and moved to Australia to pursue his passion in Geology, specifically Volcanology. He now lives in Melbourne, Australia, with his wife and son.

He has worked as a researcher and lecturer in Geosciences at Monash University, Federation University and Curtin University. He has also been one of the children's pastors at CityLife Church, Melbourne. Currently, he is on the pastoral team at Bayside Church, Melbourne, where he overseas the young adults ministry.

Jozua holds a Bachelor of Science (major: Geology) and Master of Science in Geosciences of Basins and the Lithosphere degree from the Vrije Universiteit, Amsterdam, and a Doctor of Philosophy from Monash University. He has also completed a Graduate Diploma in Theology at Harvest Bible College, Melbourne (now part of Alphacrucis College). He has published a significant number of articles in specialist journals, especially scientific, but also ministry ones. He regularly posts about his interests in both science and Christian thought on his blog.